STRONG
TOWNS

CHARLES L. MAROHN, JR.

A BOTTOM-UP REVOLUTION

STRONG TOWNS

TO REBUILD AMERICAN PROSPERITY

WILEY

Published by John Wiley & Sons, Inc., Hoboken, New Jersey.
Published simultaneously in Canada.

For general information on our other products and services or for technical support, please
contact our Customer Care Department within the United States at (800) 762-2974, outside
the United States at (317) 572–3993 or fax (317) 572-4002.

Wiley publishes in a variety of print and electronic formats and by print-on-demand. Some
material included with standard print versions of this book may not be included in e-books or
in print-on-demand. If this book refers to media such as a CD or DVD that is not included in
the version you purchased, you may download this material at http://booksupport.wiley.com.
For more information about Wiley products, visit www.wiley.com.

ISBN 9781119564812 (Hardcover)
ISBN 9781119565154 (ePDF)
ISBN 9781119564805 (ePub)

Cover Photograph: © Getty Images | Zhu Qiu / EYEEM
Cover design: Paul McCarthy

Printed in the United States of America

SKY10028793_080521

For my friend Joe, whose generosity knows no limits.
For my wife, Kirsti, whose patience is likewise endless.
And for my daughters, Chloe and Stella, who have been asked to sacrifice too much.

Contents

Foreword

Santa Ana, California, is working hard and pulling together to transform itself into a twenty-first-century city by following the advice and principles that Chuck Marohn lays out in *Strong Towns*.

I met Chuck in 2014 when he spoke in Santa Ana, California, where I served as a city council member, but I had followed Strong Towns for many years before that. Chuck's love for America's cities, and his desire to make them strong and resilient, resonated with me because that's how I felt about my city.

Thanks to my study of the Strong Towns philosophy, I have learned that cities can cultivate resiliency and prosperity in the lives of even their most vulnerable citizens. It's every elected official and public servant's responsibility to ensure we have systems in place that help cities meet the needs of their people. This book not only explains why this is so urgent, but how we get there.

For twelve years, I served on the City Council of my hometown of Santa Ana. Our community is 78 percent Latino, 10 percent Asian, and 9 percent white, with a high population of undocumented residents. It's a modern-day Ellis Island for Latinos with a median age of 29, nine years below the US median. Santa Ana, which is the fourth most densely populated city in America (right after Boston), faces all the challenges of today's urban America.

When I arrived in Santa Ana in 1990 as a young girl, I faced challenges too. My mother was in prison. I didn't know my father. My great-grandmother was raising me and eleven other great-grandchildren. We grew up in an environment with poverty, gang violence, and drugs.

I was one of the only kids who didn't use drugs, go to jail, or join a gang. I was fortunate. I had teachers and a few other adults who saw something in me and tried to help. The Boys & Girls Club of Santa Ana became my family. When I graduated high school, a businessman and community leader involved in the Boys & Girls Club offered me a job that would also pay for my education. I went to work for Mark Press at his baking company while attending the local community college. This changed my life.

I realize today that none of this would have happened without the invisible glue that binds a community together. These are the connections that are essential to a strong town.

From Chuck Marohn I came to understand how vital the physical layout of a city is for creating those connections. Strong towns aren't made by real estate speculation or self-serving public policy. They are grown by the ideas, creativity, and the imagination of people within the community and by entrepreneurs and public servants who understand what needs must be addressed for the place to prosper.

I decided to run for city council at age of 26 because I wanted to create that same sense of opportunity for others that I had been given. Nobody believed I'd win, much less make a difference, but I told my story over and over and knocked on thousands of doors. I looked people in the eye and said, "I'm not a politician. All I want to do is make a difference in the community that helped raise me." They gave me a chance, and I am grateful to say that I kept my word. I served on the Santa Ana Council from 2006 to 2018.

Like Chuck, I am a fiscal conservative and was vocal about the city being insolvent: you can't spend money you don't have. Chuck helped me understand the roots of today's public sector fiscal crisis, how we regulate real estate development in favor of auto-oriented sprawl instead of building communities that focus on mixed-use, walkable neighborhoods that emphasize social, economic, and environmental sustainability.

I became a positive disruptor, despite people who didn't want me rocking the boat. We were living in the nineteenth and twentieth centuries when Chuck came to speak to us. We had the building blocks – a street grid, a promising downtown, amazing residents, and active neighborhood associations – we just needed the right messenger to explain that we *could* make the changes we needed without leaving people behind. The Strong Towns message changed the conversation.

In the past, an alarming number of Santa Ana's residents were falling through the cracks. The standard public policy responses were based on flawed notions of what makes communities thrive. Strong Towns provides an alternative approach, one that works because it focuses on people.

Chuck believes in getting out and experiencing a community with the people who live there. It's the only way to understand where their struggles are. I saw the truth of this when I served as a volunteer policy advisor for a federal court judge who presided over a homeless case with north Orange County cities. This judge walked the six-mile riverbed stretch where more than 1,000 people were encamped. He threatened to issue an injunction and, soon after, Santa Ana built a temporary shelter in just 28 days. Within a year, we had 5 shelters in Orange County and 4 more in the pipeline.

We followed Chuck's advice in other areas too, looking for high-impact ways to make neighborhoods better for our people. Santa Ana has a very high rate of pedestrian fatalities— the third highest in the United States behind Los Angeles and San Francisco. This is an urgent matter because 56 percent of our residents don't have access to a personal car, and alternative transportation options are severely limited. We sought and received over $44 million in funding for active transportation and safety so we could address these struggles.

I stepped down from city council in 2018, but the things I fought for are still coming to fruition. We have more biking and walking infrastructure than any other city in Orange County. A streetcar is coming and promises to transform our downtown. We'll have more housing and more transportation choices, and we are creating a stronger sense of place. Such changes take time and happen incrementally, but with a Strong Towns approach, we're getting there.

When people hear the Strong Towns message, they get it. They see that we simply can't keep doing things the way we have been. Our current approach is outdated. Our governments are antiquated, with little focus on fiscal sustainability. No longer can cities experience massive growth with no way to maintain it.

A new approach will require innovation, organic co-creation of the community, transportation systems that make sense, thriving downtowns, and a commitment to taking a hard look at the math before we make decisions.

Right now, few cities have those conversations. Chuck Marohn and Strong Towns are changing that. We have the ability to rebuild our communities and create a broader prosperity. This book is your paradigm shift to get started.

Michele C. Martinez
Former City Councilmember,
City of Santa Ana, California

1

Human Habitat

For thousands of years, humans built cities for people who walked. The size of buildings, spacing of destinations, and distances individuals would travel on a routine day were scaled for a society where nearly everyone traveled by foot. This was true for human settlement across all continents, spanning all latitudes.

Today, in North America, we build cities around a more modern transportation technology: the automobile. We have developed different building types, different development styles, and different ways of arranging things on the landscape, all to accommodate a living arrangement based on automobile travel.

If you query Americans about this transition, nearly all would talk about it in terms of progress. Humans of the past used to walk everywhere and so they built settlements around people who walked. Today, we drive everywhere, and so we build our cities around people who drive. Someday people will have jet cars or teleportation technology and their cities will look completely different than ours.

The narrative we tell ourselves is one of progress. We like to think of it in this way because doing so places us on a path of improvement, one where our lives are continually getting better. There is another way to think about these changes, however, that isn't quite as comforting. It's a more plausible narrative, one worth pausing to consider.

When we ponder the layout of ancient cities, we must acknowledge that they are the byproduct of thousands of years of human tinkering. People came together in villages and tried different living arrangements. What worked, they copied and expanded. What didn't work, they discarded. That is, if those experiments hadn't already killed or disbanded them.

Humans used trial-and-error experimentation for thousands of years to refine humanity's approach to building its habitat. By the time history reaches the apex of ancient cities Americans are familiar with, places such as Athens or Rome, those experiments had been tested during times of abundance and scarcity, peace and war, disease, pestilence, stagnation, and growth. The result was a pattern of development that was adaptable, productive, and strong.

This same pattern can be seen in the pre-1900s cities of North America. While the architecture changes with geography and time, the essential layout is the same. A person living in a frontier town in the early 1900s, or Manhattan of the same period, could have bought a meal, earned a paycheck, and found a place to sleep, all within a reasonable walk. In other words, these neighborhoods would have been familiar to our ancient city-dwelling ancestors.

That same insight is no longer true. The way we now build cities in North America would be unrecognizable to an American who lived even a century ago. It would be difficult for them to comprehend a highway, a parking lot, a shopping mall, or a middle-class family in a single-family home with a three-car garage. They would be lost in the world of big box stores, office parks, and cul-de-sacs.

Get beyond whether the changes have been positive or not; there is one important aspect of this shift that is critical to acknowledge: It was abrupt. Humans had been living one way for thousands of years, yet within just a couple of decades, Americans transformed an entire continent around a new set of ideas.

Those ideas were not the byproduct of thousands of years of trial and error experimentation. They did not evolve into being. They originated largely from the writings of a handful of European intellectuals, notions their cultures largely rejected, but Americans – with lots of room, boundless optimism, and no ancient moorings – readily adopted.

In the context of human history, the North American development pattern is the largest human experiment ever attempted. In the blink of an evolutionary eye, we have transformed everything about how we live, get around, interact with each other, make decisions, conduct commerce, fall in love, and countless other aspects of human existence.

There is no going back, but there is useful wisdom we can gain from an understanding of the past.

Complex, Adaptive Systems

There are an infinite number of variables a human habitat must take into consideration. There are things we prioritize in city planning today, such as where water drains and how garbage is disposed of, but there are many other priorities that individual humans struggle to harmonize across a society.

How do we keep our food protected from potential thieves? How do we best raise our children to be acclimated to our culture? How do we take advantage of the sun to heat our house in cold weather? Where do we honorably dispose of our dead?

Each individual priority is continually weighed against the others, a balancing act of give and take across time.

Such systems are experienced as emergent. Their order is not imposed; it just appears, as if by magic. Each interaction may be understandable on its own, but the complexity of interactions makes the entire system unpredictable. Everyone learns from experience, adapts their individual behavior, and, in doing so, continuously impacts everyone else.

We often think of evolution as a process that happens incrementally over time. That's close, but the full reality is more like how Hemingway described bankruptcy: gradually, then all at once. Traumatic events, large and small, force both adaptation and failure. The combination creates the learned wisdom that is passed on to subsequent generations.

Author and philosopher Nassim Taleb has described such systems as "anti-fragile." Fragile systems degrade when stressed, but anti-fragile systems grow stronger (up to a point). We discover that it's not wise to put our village too far from the river or we'll spend too much time and energy hauling water. Later we discover that it's not wise to put our village too close to the river because a flood will wipe us out. Each of these lessons – and an infinite number of others – were learned for us, the price being our ancestors' suffering and even death.

The development pattern that was used in North America through the late 1800s represents thousands of years of received wisdom on how to build human habitat. In no way was it perfect, but it's important to understand that perfection is not possible in a system with so many competing priorities and objectives.

What is attainable is a degree of stability, the harmonious balancing of multiple things simultaneously over time. Our habitat was optimized to us, and we to our habitat. The two co-evolved. Grasping that fact opened to me a world of spooky wisdom.

Spooky Wisdom

I had the opportunity to spend time in Italy during my mid-20s. Walking amid the ruins of Pompeii, I noted a little shop that had served as the fast food restaurant of its day. It was located on one of the direct paths from the core of the city to the edge, although it was closer to the outskirts than the center of the action.

The building was small: just two rooms. The room furthest from the street was the living quarters, closed at the back but with an opening to the front. The front room along the street was where the food was kept warm and dispensed out of pots placed under a countertop. The countertop ran along the sidewalk for ease of service.

As an engineer who had worked on site layout and project development for a handful of fast food restaurants, my initial reaction was: how quaint. Look at how these simple people lived. What a hard and miserable life. Thank goodness we are so much more intelligent and sophisticated today. Thank goodness we have risen above this.

In subsequent years, I would grow to realize how ignorant I had been.

With just two rooms, the family member who ran the fast food operation in front could also keep an eye on small kids in back, taking a break from sales when times were slow and being more attentive when they were not. Thus, half the household's parents could both create an income stream and care for young family members simultaneously.

This freed up the other half of the household, along with any extended family that lived under the roof, to get a job elsewhere, likely outside of the city doing some form of manual labor. Matthew 20: 1–16, in the New Testament, relays the Parable of the Workers, describing how people would line up in the marketplace to be selected for manual labor. This was a common arrangement of the day, with those selected earning a day's wages.

What this family had created was income diversity. If no labor was to be had that day, hopefully the restaurant would provide some fallback income. If the restaurant had a slow day, ideally it was because there were wages to be had laboring in vineyards. If both had a successful day, it allowed some savings to accrue for those times when both sources of income dried up.

A stretch of good fortune for both income streams would cause savings to grow into a nest egg, some real wealth that could be used to improve the family's situation. Maybe they used that wealth to expand the restaurant. Or to hire help, perhaps purchasing a slave culled from the ranks of a defeated enemy, which was common practice. Again, I'm not describing a utopia; I'm describing a complex system that imperfectly harmonizes many competing priorities simultaneously over time.

What is important is that the strategies emerging in such systems are anti-fragile. They limit the risk of catastrophe while maintaining the capacity for improvement, particularly during stress events. These are the strategies that survive the test of time, and when it comes to the Pompeii fast food restaurant, I'm just getting started.

The building was located near the edge of town. The land was likely acquired for free or at a very low price. Prime real estate near the center of town would have been much more expensive, but on the edge, someone could start with relatively nothing. Yet, if the community grew and prospered, the edge would expand outward. The shop owner would then find themselves with an investment now strategically located closer to the center, a more valuable situation.

The little shop owner thus shared a common fate with other property owners in the city. It was not a zero-sum game, where one benefits only at the expense of others. I'm not suggesting they all lived in harmony, but they had a lot of selfish incentives for altruism.

This makes the common walls of the buildings more understandable. The Pompeii fast-food structure shared a wall with its neighbor on each side. We can appreciate the lawyers and building inspectors involved with something like this today, but historically, shared walls were the norm. Common walls meant shared cost, an advantage when you were short on resources. It also meant that heat would dissipate more slowly in cold seasons, reducing fuel consumption.

With buildings sharing common walls and having their sole entrance face the street, the place was made more secure for everyone. Someone wanting to enter a home for nefarious reasons would be subject to the random watchful gaze of neighbors, both during an approach and upon exit. Even in cities where there was a paid security force, this design was a way to provide a decent amount of security at a marginal cost.

To the extent that human and animal waste in the streets allowed, the street itself was a place for people to gather, including neighborhood children. Shared parenting – I'll watch your kid and you watch mine – took the strain off raising kids who were too old to be kept in the home, but not yet old enough to work.

The building itself was very simple, just a two-room box. It's easy to see that if things didn't work out with the restaurant, the building could be adapted to a new use. Or, if things worked out really well, the neighboring building could be acquired and the two merged together. If sometime in the future that arrangement no longer worked, the buildings could be easily subdivided again. The inherent flexibility meant that people didn't need to be able to project what would happen in the future to act today; they just built structures that could be adapted to harmonize changing priorities.

The collection of buildings on either side of the fast food restaurant were built in a line. They faced a mirrored set of buildings on the opposite side of the street, also in a line. These opposite rows of buildings were spaced at ratios comfortable to human beings. They were not so close as to feel constrained, but they were not so far that they failed to create an edge.

Edges are very important for humans. In our habitats, we are drawn to edges. This is a phenomenon observed by Jane Jacobs in her book *The Death and Life of Great American Cities*, then elaborated on by Christopher Alexander in *A Pattern Language*. In public spaces, Jacobs notes that people "stay to the sides," while Alexander states that people "naturally gravitate toward the edge." This street in Pompeii provided that opportunity.

Biologists call this wall-hugging trait *thigmotaxis*. Think of a mouse scurrying along the edge of a wall, instinctively fearful of journeying into the center of the room. Humans have that same propensity. Darwin called evolution a "conservative process" in that it conserves winning strategies and builds on them. At some point in the very distant past, thigmotaxis was a winning strategy. The alignment of the buildings along the street in Pompeii comforted that primal urge.

In the book *Cognitive Architecture*, Ann Sussman and Justin B. Hollander explore how humans respond to the habitats they have built for themselves. They explore thigmotaxis, but they also dig into a phenomenon called *pareidolia*, the propensity for humans to find faces in objects. When people see Elvis or the Virgin Mary in a piece of burnt toast, they are experiencing pareidolia.

Faces trigger a strong emotional response in humans. Sussman and Hollander quote the Danish architect Jan Gehl in suggesting, "Man is man's greatest joy," that people delight in seeing other people. As written in *Cognitive Architecture*:

> Our face-sensing capability is so strong and present that faces also appear to be put into building elevations or facades unintentionally. It reflects the fact some researchers believe pareidolia, the subconscious tendency to assemble faces in random objects, plays a much more significant role in design, aesthetics, and our appreciation of buildings and cityscapes than is generally realized.[1]

The Pompeii restaurant has the rough proportions of a face; it is narrower than it is tall (Figure 1.1). Contrast this with the

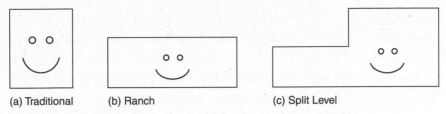

(a) Traditional   (b) Ranch   (c) Split Level

Figure 1.1 (a) Traditional home with proportions of a face. Neither the (b) ranch home nor the (c) split-level home has face-like proportions.

rough proportions of a 1950s ranch home or a 1990s split-level home. In trying to build something functional that would simultaneously add to human delight, the builders in Pompeii made the most out of meager resources.

They almost certainly also employed symmetry in the building's exterior design and symmetrical shapes in the ornamentation. This is because, as Sussman and Hollander point out, humans have a natural disposition toward symmetry. We not only process symmetrical designs more quickly than nonsymmetrical ones, but:

> Researchers have also learned that looking at symmetrical objects subconsciously activates our smiling muscles more than looking at random patterns. And when we smile, we are more likely to feel calm or reassured.[2]

Why do humans see beauty in symmetry? Sussman and Hollander suggest it is for the same reason we have our other subconscious traits: "It is bound up and cannot be teased apart from survival."

A Pompeii street lined with shops and homes, each designed to convey humans through town in the most comforting and pleasant way that could be attained while still harmonizing many other urgent needs, provides the perfect framing for a monumental building or even a simple public gathering space.

Think of the way that a great picture frame draws out the magnificence of the picture. When buildings line up to form a wall, they serve as a frame. The picture is whatever sits at the termination point of the street; it's naturally drawn out, whatever magnificence it has magnified by the framing.

The termination point could be a place of worship, a fountain, a park, a civic building, or even the house of a wealthy family. In the case of Pompeii, the street terminated at the Forum, the center of Roman life. This arrangement served to draw out Roman values and culture into the broader community, connecting the day-to-day lives of Pompeii's citizens with the broader society in which they lived.

This design is not by accident. In his book *The Original Green*, architect Steve Mouzon describes the elements of making a place lovable, which he suggests is a key component of building cities that endure. Loveable places reflect us; we see ourselves and our common culture within them. They delight us with beauty and comfort. And they harmonize us with nature and the rhythms of life. This design worked to accomplish all three.

I could go on this way for a long time. Suffice it to say, the little building in Pompeii was more than a mere restaurant and home. It was one component of an evolving human ecosystem. That habitat helped the people of Pompeii meet their daily needs, but it also helped them raise their young, care for their elderly, save for the future, pass along their stories and culture, comfort their primal urges, and reach for higher truths by communing with the existential. In short, the city helped make them human.

We are compelled today to acknowledge that the wisdom contained in the cities our ancestors built, in the patterns and approaches they developed over thousands of years, exceeds our capacity to fully understand. There are deeper truths there than we will ever know, spooky wisdom that has co-evolved along with humanity itself, to serve our needs – known and unknown – in ways we have been far too eager to casually dismiss.

Systems That Are Merely Complicated

As an engineer, I'm trained to see cities as a collection of roads, streets, pipes, pumps, valves, and meters. My education as a planner provided some additional depth in the realm of economics, land use, and the environment, but the knowledge gained was still superficial. The practice of city planning has largely been reduced to zoning, a way of categorizing the world into homogenous blocks, primarily for ease of regulation and transportation, the latter being the primary way we facilitate growth within our cities.

What both professions have in common is that they view cities as complicated, but not complex. There is a massive difference, and it's critical to explaining why our modern cities are so fragile.

Something that is complicated can have many moving parts, but those parts are ultimately knowable, understandable, and predictable. A mechanical watch is complicated. It has many gears and switches that interact in ways that only highly trained watchmakers understand. Even so, a watchmaker can tell you what will happen to one gear if a different gear is moved.

The watch is merely complicated because it lacks the ability to adapt. The gears in a watch can receive information in the form of stress, but they can only respond as they are designed. They can't change their approach, or adapt to a new set of stressors in novel ways. A watch is incapable of evolving.

Most importantly, systems that are complicated are fragile. They don't get stronger when subjected to stressors. They can't adapt, so they can only become weaker. With time being infinite, every complicated system will eventually fail.

When humans imagine cities as complicated machines and not complex human habitat, they fail to grasp what is really happening. They misdiagnose problems and opportunities as being a byproduct of one or two related variables, instead of one manifestation of an interrelated, complex system. Our responses – often as disproportionately overwhelming as they are rote – stifle adaptation and, in doing so, unintentionally increase fragility.

So why are we stuck seeing our cities as merely complicated? Why can't our professionals, policymakers, and citizens at large grasp the complexity?

Our modern development pattern – a continental-scale social experiment – was established during a period of unprecedented abundance after World War II. We were not only the sole economic superpower that wasn't devastated by war; the biggest players in the world were indebted to us. We held the global reserve currency, we had the greatest amount of easily accessible oil and coal resources, and we had a generation of motivated young people culturally unified by shared hardship and common enemies.

All the systems that launched this massive experiment, from the new financing mechanisms to the highway and infrastructure programs, were developed at a unique period of time when we could dream big and accomplish anything. For a moment, our vision was not constrained by our reach.

For complex systems, an abundance of resources destroys the need for adaptation. It renders the complex merely complicated. This effect is described by Neil Johnson in his book *Simply Complexity*:

> Why is competition for limited resources so important in real-world systems? The answer is simple. In real-world situations where there is no competition, it matters little what decisions people actually make. In other words, if there is an over-supply of desirable resources, then it doesn't matter very much what we decide to do since we will still have enough of everything we need, and more.
>
> In such situations, we could each go around acting in whatever way we wanted, either cleverly or stupidly, and yet still end up with an embarrassment of riches. Hence there is no need to learn from the past, or adapt. The need for feedback then becomes pretty meaningless since we are all getting what we want all the time.
>
> The end result is that the collection of objects in question will behave in a fairly simple way. In particular, the lack of dependence on any feedback or interactions between the objects will make the overall system non-complex.[3]

The underlying assumption of the American development pattern is an abundance of resources. When this was essentially true in the decades immediately after World War II, our cities functioned in ways that were complicated, but not complex. We could, as Johnson suggested, act "cleverly or stupidly, and yet still end up with an embarrassment of riches." And we did.

Have a crime problem? Just hire more police. There's no real incentive to design homes to face the street, to have front porches and windows that open onto the common space, to provide a base level of self-policing in a neighborhood. That would require a sacrifice of some privacy. It would force people to work cooperatively, to learn to rely on their neighbors. We have the resources, so just hire some more officers.

Have a traffic congestion problem? Just build more lanes. There is no incentive to minimize auto trips, to create neighborhoods where people can walk or bike for most of their daily needs. That would involve changing zoning codes, allowing people to start businesses in neighborhoods where they are currently prohibited, and maybe even increasing the cost of driving during peak times. We have the money, so just build more capacity.

Are sales at the big box store stagnating? Just close it and build a new one in a better location. There is no incentive to construct buildings that can serve multiple purposes or be easily adapted to another use. Achieving that resiliency would compel our economy to be less efficient and our transactions more localized, and that would change the nature of growth in our economy. So long as profit is to be made building a new store, we would be foolish to stop it from happening.

Experiencing an increase in the teen suicide rate? An epidemic of obesity? Out-of-control costs for senior medical care? No matter the problem, and no matter how bad it becomes, there is no force compelling us to evolve our habitat, to change the way we live together. Each challenge has become but a complicated problem to be worked out by someone else, through public policy or market mechanisms. We're the wealthiest nation in the history of mankind, after all.

In our new experimental living pattern, feedback and adaptation have become meaningless. We do not perceive any need for our human habitat to harmoniously balance multiple things simultaneously. Why would we when we can just go ahead and use our resources to solve problems as we become aware of them?

This approach worked well right after World War II – perhaps too well. It allowed Americans to, for a time, address many of civilization's nagging struggles. Through our success, however, we collectively developed a low tolerance for uncomfortable feedback and a reduction in our ability to adapt to stress.

We're more comfortable behaving as if our cities are merely complicated. Increasingly, they are not.

Notes

1. Ann Sussman and Justin B. Hollander, *Cognitive Architecture: Designing For How We Respond to the Built Environment* (New York: Routledge, 2015).
2. Ibid.
3. Neil Johnson, *Simply Complexity: A Clear Guide to Complexity Theory* (London: Oneworld Publications, 2017).

2

Incremental Growth

Take a tentative step in the dark. If you do not run into something, you just gained knowledge. If you hit a wall, the incremental nature of your advance gives you wisdom without much lost.

Now take an abrupt leap in the dark. The gain may come at a more rapid pace, but the risk of breaking your nose is far greater. Even if successful, it is unlikely you can repeat this trick many times without serious calamity.

When there are an unknowable number of variables and feedback loops that react to and ultimately impact what we do, and when calamity is not an outcome we are willing to risk, the way to probe uncertainty is through incremental change. This is exactly the approach embodied in the traditional development pattern.

Complex, adaptive systems grow incrementally. That is the method they use to simultaneously harmonize multiple competing interests, to learn – through experimentation – what truly works and what doesn't.

Each part of the system receives feedback to changes as they happen. Each part responds to positive and negative stressors, adaptations that impact every other part of the system. It is an approach predicated upon failure – preferably small, early failures – as a path to wisdom.

My hometown of Brainerd, Minnesota, was founded in the years immediately following the Civil War. There is a photo I obtained through our historical society that shows an early iteration (Figure 2.1). It's a series of little pop-up shacks arranged in a line next to the train stop. The buildings are all nondescript, single-story, wood structures with minimal ornamentation. When I look at them, I see a series of little bets my ancestors made, generations ago – nothing colossal, nothing monumental, just things that might succeed or fail. The outcome of any single bet wouldn't prove decisive.

Looking at this photo, it's clear what happened. Some lumberjacks and speculators, looking for a place they could start

Figure 2.1 Front Street in Brainerd, Minnesota, 1870

modestly and build successfully, got off the train in the middle of a forest at a spot where the railroad crossed the Mississippi river. They cut down some of the trees and planed them out for lumber. With the materials they had on hand and copying a pattern they had seen work in other places, they built those little shacks, the first iteration of a city.

This is how every city in human history up to this point had begun: a series of pop-up shacks, some hopes, and some dreams. The great cities of North America – San Francisco, Chicago, Houston, and Manhattan – all began in this way. London, Paris, Milan, and the cities of Europe, likewise. Even ancient cities, where urban DNA was in a more infantile phase, places like Alexandria, Thebes, Beirut, and Damascus, were founded in this same manner.

In North America, we built thousands of such places. For a variety of complex reasons that defy our ability to predict, project, or even fully understand after-the-fact, many of these places failed. Some combination of the wrong people, the wrong place, and the wrong time conspired to thwart those hopes and dreams. The many prerequisites needed to make it successful just didn't come together.

It's important to understand what happens when a place like this fails – not much. A few people suffer some, they salvage what they can, and they move on. I'm not trying to diminish their individual pain; rather, my intent is to point out the isolation of that pain from the larger society. When a place like this fails, there is no corresponding nationwide spike in unemployment. The stock market doesn't crash. We don't need an emergency bailout of Wall Street banks lest there be no food on the nation's grocery shelves in a couple days. These are small, isolated bets, an opportunity to gain knowledge at low risk. In the overall scheme of things, their failure at this early stage is survivable. In fact, it's better to fail early when the stakes are low.

In North America, we started thousands of cities as a collection of little pop-up shacks. For a variety of complex reasons that defy our ability to predict, project, or even fully understand after-the-fact, many of these places were successful. The combination of people, place, and time came together in a way that worked. When it did, something simple to comprehend, yet altogether magical, began to happen.

The city would grow. It would incrementally grow outward, incrementally grow upward, and incrementally become more intense. In time, the row of pop-up shacks is replaced with a collection of buildings that are more substantial investments. And the edge of town, where there once was bare ground or sparse settlement, is the next iteration of the pop-up shack, a small experiment to discover the next generation of success.

In the case of my hometown, the next photo of the same street comes 34 years after the first (Figure 2.2). The shacks are gone and in their place are two- and three-story wood structures. In another 40 years, those wood buildings would be replaced by buildings of brick and granite.

A core characteristic of growing complex, adaptive systems is the incremental nature of the growth. The pace can be fast

Figure 2.2 Front Street in Brainerd, Minnesota, 1904

or glacially slow, but either way, change happens through many tentative steps in the dark. Historically, cities have grown incrementally on a continuum of improvement. Start with a pop-up shack and eventually get to Manhattan.

The key difference between historic development patterns and the way Americans began to build cities in the twentieth century is our capacity to skip the messy iterations and jump to what we perceive to be the perfect end. Today, we build in large leaps, and we build to a finished state. We envision the end condition – for a building, a block, or a neighborhood – and that is what we go forth and create.

When we build it, we are then done. There is no anticipation of change, incremental or otherwise. The building won't adapt, the block won't evolve, and the neighborhood won't transform over time, at least not easily. As it is built, evermore will it be, world without end. This commitment to stasis requires a level of cultural hubris bordering on the absurd, particularly given the pace of change we've grown used to in all parts of our society.

Humans are not good at predicting the future. This is a lesson our ancestors grew to understand over thousands of years of living together in evolving cities. We don't know what will happen next year, or in a decade, or a century from now. Things change. Our needs change. In a world of limits, one where we can't just overcome our mistakes by expending endless resources, the way to avoid the fatal flaw is to build things that are adaptable, that can evolve to serve multiple purposes.

In a world without limits, there is no cost for guessing wrong. We can simply tear down and rebuild each failure, applying cultural narratives to explain to ourselves why no reasonable person could have seen that mistake coming. There is no real cost so long as there are adequate resources to overcome mistakes, or mistakes impact parts of society that can be ignored or rationalized away. Ultimately, it doesn't really matter what is built or what resources we expend in building it.

That is the difference between experiencing the city as merely complicated instead of complex. It's also the reason why modern Americans insist it is possible to predict the future, even though humans have proven over and over that, with complex systems, it is not.

Complex versus Complicated Buildings

Complexity happened in residential neighborhoods in the same way it happened with the pop-up shacks near the railroad stop. Many traditional neighborhoods began with what we would today call a tiny home, something currently illegal in many cities. A 600-square-foot box – a 20-foot by 30-foot simple structure – could have a kitchen and dining room, a living room, bedroom, and a bath. Very simple, but also affordable, especially when built on cheaper land on the edge of town.

Visit many American neighborhoods established before the 1920s and you can still witness many of these structures, although likely not in their infant phase. That's because they are designed to evolve, to be added on to and changed to suit different needs.

Have a child? Build an addition on the back. Have a second child? Build another story. Need extra income? Create a basement entrance and rent out the lower-level space. Have a business idea? Convert the front of the home to a shop or office. Able to save some money? Change the front stoop into a full porch.

There are an endless set of permutations that can be brought forth from the simple box, all based on the changing needs and resources of the time. Without tearing down the original structure, a home of this type could be modified to serve an individual, a family, or even multiple families. It could be a home for someone with modest means or someone who is affluent. Once established, a traditional neighborhood can always be adapted to new needs.

And critical to the way communities grow stronger over time, this approach allowed people to start with relatively little and incrementally build that into real wealth. This is all in sharp contrast to the way Americans build neighborhoods today.

Today we build individual homes, as well as complete neighborhoods, all at once, to a finished state. There is no starting small and adding on as resources allow; property is purchased using long-term financing sold into a secondary market, with banks and insurers requiring a finished product as a prerequisite to completing the transaction.

Standardization of the core product and assembly methods has made the home-building process hyper-efficient, theoretically driving down the cost per square foot. The price of a home has not gone down, however; the amount of square feet per structure has merely gone up.[1] Financing mechanisms force home builders to build to a final state, and they force buyers to enter the market with a fully mature home at a high price point. The true entry-level product has been squeezed out.

Along with a higher bar to entry, zoning and building regulations keep things from evolving. Regardless of need or changing circumstance, modern zoning codes typically don't allow single-family homes to be converted into multi-family, not even to rent out a room to a college student for some extra cash. Same with adding a business. Even if the market demand is there, zoning regulations might allow some limited home occupations, but nothing that would betray the residential uniformity of the neighborhood.

Zoning, as well as land covenants and property associations, create uniformity across each new neighborhood that is built. Not only are all homes on a given cul-de-sac built within a few years of each other, they are all built in a tight price range. Homes are clustered together by price, with a buffer between them and homes in a different price point.

Homes for the modestly wealthy, or those who can make the payments of a modestly wealthy family, are in a completely different pod from homes for the very wealthy, even though they are both wealthy by American standards. Those pods are disconnected from each other and separated by buffers, as if someone driving a Lexus would be injured by living in proximity to someone merely driving a Buick. This kind of stratification happens for all classes of society.

Modern city-building efficiently creates pods of static, monoculture development. As ecosystems, monocultures are inherently fragile. The fragility of the American development pattern is amplified by the unnatural stasis imposed: the inability to adapt to changing circumstances.

When we build a neighborhood all at once to a finished state, we have – at best – a moment of perfection, a period of time when everything works as envisioned. But even in the most perfect development, an unavoidable, yet entirely predictable, stress looms.

The homes were all built at the same time; they will all reach the end of their life cycle at the same time. Within the lifetime of the mortgage debt for the home, the homes in the neighborhood will simultaneously start to fail.

An asphalt-shingled roof will last for 25 to 30 years, and then it will need to be replaced. Because they were all built at the same time, every home in the neighborhood will need a new roof within a few years of each other. Failure to maintain the roof has serious consequences; a modern chipboard and sheetrock home will go bad quickly with a failed roof.

The siding of every home in the neighborhood will also fail at roughly the same time. Everyone's appliances will go bad within a few years of each other. The sidewalks and driveways will crack and be overgrown with weeds, all at the same time. Building a neighborhood all at once, instead of incrementally, merely ensures that all the inevitable pressures of decline will occur simultaneously across the entire neighborhood.

And because the neighborhood is built to a finished state, because no higher use is anticipated or even allowed on the property, the only available options are stagnation and decline. In the best-case scenario, the buildings will be maintained as they are, regardless of the cost or return on investment for doing so, and the neighborhood will stagnate, not improving but not getting worse.

The more likely scenario is that, as the signs of decline start to become apparent, the more affluent in the neighborhood will move. They will do the logical thing and sell their home in the declining neighborhood and purchase another in a neighborhood they perceive to be a better investment. That will leave people with lesser financial means to struggle to maintain homes within a deteriorating neighborhood.

Ultimately the relentless pressure of time and entropy will push the neighborhood into decline. It may take a few years or a few decades, but all possible futures converge on the sole remaining outcome: decline. It's like treading water, a binary set of outcomes – stagnation or decline – and there is no easy path back once the cycle of decline is established.

Neighborhood Renewal

The incremental approach to building neighborhoods contains a natural rejuvenation mechanism, introducing a third variable to the otherwise depressing menu of stagnation and decline: renewal. Traditional development drives renewal by improving the underlying value of land.

The value of all developed property has two components: the value of the land and the value of the improvements on the land.

Property Value = Improvement Value + Land Value

There is a relationship between the improvement value and the land value, a ratio at which an improvement makes sense given the land value. Consider two extreme instances to illustrate the point.

Manhattan real estate is extremely valuable. If there is any raw land in Manhattan, it would be some of the most expensive square footage in North America. It would be unthinkable – and not very stable over time – for someone to purchase prime real estate in Manhattan and place a mobile home on it. The absurdity of putting such a low value improvement on such expensive real estate is obvious. The highest and best use, as real estate purveyors like to describe it, is much greater.

Conversely, real estate in the second and third rings around Detroit is extremely cheap. Raw land can be acquired for far below the cost of the infrastructure that has already been provided to the site, suggesting the land actually has negative value in some places. It would be very strange for someone to buy a single lot in one of these neighborhoods and put a $10 million luxury home on it. The value of the land would not support such an investment. While it is possible that this kind of investment might happen sometime and someplace, it would be an outlier event, an exception to the rule, and not part of a general pattern of development.

Stated simply, there is a ratio of improvement value to land value that is stable. If that ratio gets too low – a situation where the land is valuable compared to the improvement on it – redevelopment pressure increases. A cheap improvement on an expensive piece of land is a prime candidate for redevelopment. Someone is likely to buy the property, demolish the existing structures, and build something new, something of higher intensity that would more closely justify the higher land value.

An expensive improvement on a cheap piece of land is likely to raise the value of the land, not just on the site of the improvement but on neighboring properties. This is especially true if the improvement is built in such a way that it complements surrounding properties.

These two realities – rising land prices inducing redevelopment, redevelopment increasing land values – work together in an incremental framework of development to create a natural renewal mechanism within a neighborhood (Figure 2.3).

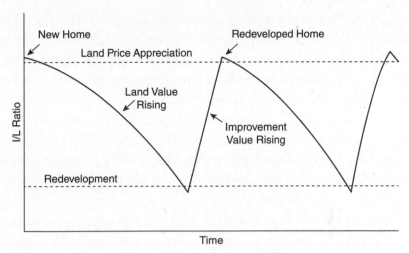

Figure 2.3   Improvement to Land (I/L) Ratio over Time

Low I/L Ratio: Redevelopment
High I/L Ratio: Land Price Appreciation

Consider the row of pop-up shacks described earlier, the starting point for every city built before modern times. When those shacks were originally constructed, the land was cheap. So were the shacks. No early speculator went into a frontier town like mine and, before anything else had been constructed, built a bank with granite columns and marble stairs. That would have been silly. The town could easily have become a ghost town and that massive investment would be lost.

The first iteration of every city was cheap buildings on cheap land. Little bets.

With every cheap building that went in, however, the value of the land increased. A row of shacks constitutes a place, somewhere people from the surrounding area could come to have a drink, purchase supplies, cable the outside world, meet other people, play billiards, and go to church. Each new building, each new enterprise, improved the value of the place.

This is especially true with the traditional design as it had evolved. These shacks were built in a tight cluster for a reason;

their proximity to each other created value for all of them. This could be enhanced, even in really poor places, by the design. This first iteration of a city began the process of harmonizing multiple objectives, one of them being the urgent need to make the place valuable enough to endure.

Each individual property owner, acting in their own self-interest, would do what is best for themselves. Yet, even in an infant phase of development, this highly evolved human habitat would harmonize those selfish actions to the benefit of the other, nearby property owners.

If a property owner in this early phase of a town wanted to maximize their own position, they would build their building in line with the others on the street. They would have their entrance and windows facing the street. They would make the front of their building as ornate as resources and skill would allow. They would put the trash and latrine and other less-savory things in the rear of the building, away from potential patrons.

Each of these things, and more I'm certainly overlooking, would improve their own property's value. It would also increase the value of adjacent properties. The traditional way of building – the way they would have all intuitively understood as the only proper way to do things – used individual action to maximize the collective value of the place. This is one of those spooky features of complex systems.

And it is a critical feature, because improving the collective value of the place is a requirement if the city is to become stronger and more prosperous. It is a prerequisite for the survival of the town. North America is full of failed settlements, most long forgotten, that didn't successfully meet this viability threshold.

As the block of pop-up shacks is developed, as those small investments are growing into a place, the land underneath each of those shacks increases in value. Simultaneous with the rising land values, the shacks themselves are declining. The owners of these shacks, which were hastily constructed of rather marginal materials anyway, must put resources and energy into maintaining them if they want them to retain their value. If they don't make those maintenance investments, their buildings will start to decline. This condition – rising land values and declining improvement values – accelerates redevelopment pressure.

At some point, someone will purchase that property, tear down the shack, and build something more substantive, something that better aligns with the underlying value of the land. So long as the underlying land continues to rise in value – so long as the place continues to get better – this redevelopment pressure will exist, transforming buildings that go into decline into investment opportunities.

This is how a street transforms from pop-up shack to two- and three-story wood structures. This is the mechanism used to nudge that second-generation street into one with buildings of brick and granite. And this is the way a well-situated little town grew from a tiny settlement into Manhattan: incrementally, on a continuum of improvement, with the resulting increase in land values creating a self-reinforcing renewal process.

The Stifling Nature of High Land Values

This renewal process might seem like a wonderful thing, particularly compared to the cycle of decline we experience in modern cities, so it's important to reiterate that evolution is not a happy process. Adaptation happens in response to stress. Complex systems are relentless in forcing failure, as early and conclusively as possible. There are good reasons Americans abandoned this approach after World War II when they had the opportunity, turning their back in the process on millennia of accumulated wisdom in pursuit of something they felt to be better.

Auto-oriented, suburban development was an attempt to address many problems with the city. One of the most pernicious was the stifling nature of high land values, the inevitable result of a maturing city.

A key characteristic of traditional cities, especially those that reached a level of maturity, was stability. These were human habitats designed to endure, a refinement achieved through thousands of years of trial and error experimentation. In a coarse sense, a traditional city is valuable land surrounded by cheap land, wealthy people surrounded by poor people. The stability of the city was a function of this wealth.

For young cities, this relationship between the center and the edge was a feature. An upstart could acquire cheap land on the nearby edge of the city, make a nominal investment of largely sweat equity, and experience the increase in wealth of a rising tide. This allowed people to start with nothing and end up with something, to start small and share in the prosperity of the community as the human habitat matured.

The more mature the city, however, the more entrenched the wealth. This is great for the stability of the community as communal efforts, such as police protection or water distribution, require a stable base of wealth to draw from. It was less appreciated by those who had nothing, who found themselves living in places that had matured, where the opportunities incremental improvement provides had slowed.

Auto-oriented development changes this dynamic radically. When a connection is made between two places – by a river or a railroad or a highway – that connection creates value for each place. It builds wealth. The original vision for America's highways was for them to function as connections between established places, to augment the wealth creation mechanism of rivers and railroads. Had that been done, it would have reinforced existing development patterns further entrenching the stifling nature of high land values.

Instead, all levels of American government coalesced around policies that destroyed the underlying land values of core cities. The mechanism is simple: Running a road through the center of an established neighborhood to the edge of town opens land up for development. With the automobile and the new road, comparatively massive amounts of raw land is now reachable. From a simple supply and demand standpoint, flooding the market with cheap land drives down the price of land.

Instead of connecting places, highways primarily became a mechanism for land development around our cities. Policies were established at the state and federal levels focusing on auto-commuting patterns. Highways were run, not around cities, but through the middle of established neighborhoods. Cities adopted regulations and practices – such as high design speeds on local streets, parking requirements for private property, and anti-walking campaigns – that privilege distant auto-commuters over local land owners. Over time, mitigating traffic congestion became a top public policy priority.

This is not great for those wealthy property owners who experienced the destruction of their property values in the core of the city, but it was great for people suffering under an approach that favors high land values, particularly middle-class families that couldn't get into the prime real estate. Coming after the Great Depression and World War II, this flipping of the economic chessboard was exactly what Americans were looking for.

Even so, this shift was a disaster for the financial stability of the community, which depends on extracting wealth to provide for ongoing communal services. The next chapter will examine how local governments have responded by shifting from an approach centered around wealth creation to one dependent on increasing rates of growth.

Simultaneous with highway building and the government-led creation of auto-oriented suburbs came the destruction of property values in the core of every American city. Again, with supply and demand dynamics, a massive increase in developable land puts downward pressure on land prices. With underlying land values in mature neighborhoods not just stagnant but falling, the natural renewal mechanism that gave cities stability collapsed.

In the subsequent decades, buildings of astounding grandeur in our core cities were razed to make room for parking lots.
It wasn't because parking provides great value – it doesn't – but
merely that the cost of maintaining and repairing the structures
could not be justified with collapsing land values. Americans
spent an incredible amount of money to destroy generations of
wealth, buildings of such magnificence that we could not recre-
ate them today if we desired to.

Modern development is built all at once and to a finished
state, a condition that does not naturally induce the rising
land values necessary to drive redevelopment and renewal. We
have defeated the stifling constraint of high land values, but in
exchange we sacrificed the stability that has been the hallmark of
cities throughout time.

Private and Public Investment

Consider the pop-up shacks of Brainerd once again, only this
time ponder the public infrastructure serving them. In short,
there was none. There were no sewer and water systems. No
streets or sidewalks. No drainage system. Nothing. The first iteration of the city didn't produce enough wealth to justify any of
those things. The people who built that place had more urgent
things to do with their resources.

The second generation of buildings was different. Along
with those two- and three-story wood structures came a
wooden sidewalk and a gravel street. The modest increase in
wealth justified and supported the modest increase in collective commitment.

The third generation of brick and granite buildings had
fully modern infrastructure systems. There were concrete sidewalks on the edges of an asphalt street. A storm drain is visible
in the middle of the street, a way to shed rainwater into a pipe
that would also transport sewage to the river. There is a fire
hydrant on the corner indicating a water system. The increase

in intensity of the street supported an increase in intensity of communal infrastructure.

That little collection of pop-up shacks did not produce enough wealth to maintain a paved street or a sewer and water system, even if they had somehow found the money to build it. The community that could afford to build brick and granite buildings could also afford to build and maintain all those infrastructure systems; there was enough wealth there to extract what was necessary to keep it all going.

There is no chicken and egg conundrum here; in traditional cities, private investment preceded public investment. The wealth of the private investment is necessary to justify, and ultimately sustain, the collective public investment. This is essential for community stability. Evolved systems punish failure; they use little bets to probe uncertainty, but never ongoing gambling as a pathway to prosperity.

For traditional cities, rising private wealth leads to increased public commitment. The city itself serves as the ultimate rentier, extracting ongoing income from the wealth of the community, for the benefit of the community. The stable relationship between private and public investment graphs as shown in Figure 2.4.

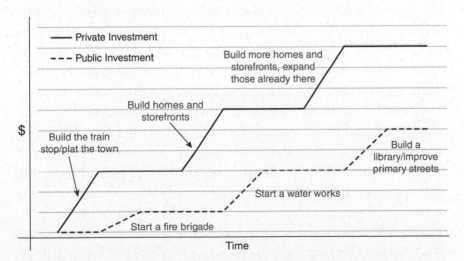

Figure 2.4 Private Investment Leading Public Investment

This is in stark contrast to everything we experience today regarding growth and development. Instead of private wealth leading, in today's cities it is the collective public investment that leads. Governments frequently invest millions of dollars, or make long-term maintenance commitments worth millions, before any taxable private investment has been made.

In the best-case scenario for a local government, a developer will agree to put in all the required public infrastructure – all the roads, streets, curbs, sidewalks, pipes, pumps, valves, and meters – and do so completely at their own expense. The developer takes the first life-cycle risk, the chance that the development does not cash flow adequately enough to cover the up-front expense. What the city then assumes is the ongoing maintenance liability and the risk that the development will not grow to have, or retain over time, adequate tax base to fund ongoing maintenance costs. This is the best deal our cities ever experience today. Most cities do far worse.

For example, in addition to the long-term maintenance costs, some cities voluntarily incur financing risk during the development process. They serve as the bank for the developer by borrowing the money to build new infrastructure, using the good faith and credit of their taxpayers as security. The developer, in exchange, agrees to pay back the loan, with some interest, when the developed property sells, although sometimes that promise is transferred to the property owner at the time of purchase. Either way, the city is taking the additional risk that the development fails, in which case they are stuck with the debt, a nonperforming asset and the long-term maintenance liability.

Some cities will forego working with a private developer altogether and simply acquire and develop the property themselves. The concept of a shovel-ready site, owned by the city and ready for transfer, with all the public utilities preinstalled, has become commonplace. These deals are often sweetened with tax subsidies, waiving of fees, and expedited permitting.

While these approaches are commonplace today, it's important to recognize the shift in phasing and risk that has occurred.

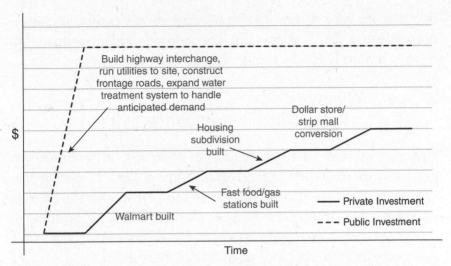

Figure 2.5   Public Investment Leading Private Investment

Instead of private investment leading, the public sector now takes the risks by being out in front of the development process. The modern relationship between public and private investment is graphed as shown in Figure 2.5.

None of this is to suggest that, throughout human history prior to modern times, the public sector never took risk to spur development. They did; it was just the rare occasion and not the rule. Today, the public sector backstops almost all private land development, either by direct investments up front or by assuming the long-term maintenance obligations before the tax base has matured.

While this might seem like a subtle shift, the impacts are enormous. Once in place, public infrastructure investments become sunk costs. Cities have the capacity to borrow large sums of money, or shortchange other parts of their budget, to make debt payments. This blunts the intensely motivating incentive of financial failure and replaces it with the more abstract notion of political failure.

When the public sector leads, vacant space becomes an embarrassment instead of an immediate fiscal crisis. The human need to fill the space, at whatever cost, is not conducive to good decision-making. Worst of all, putting all the public improvements into a finished state before any private investment has occurred merely ensures that the city will become a bad party.

The Party Analogy

Consider a dinner party where each invited guest brings more food and beverage than they themselves consume. With each person that shows up, there is a wider selection of food and drink, the conversation grows, and the party simply gets better. The logical thing to do as host of this good party is to open the doors as wide as possible and invite more people in. The more the merrier!

What about a party where each invited guest consumes more food and beverage than they themselves bring to the party? With each person that shows up, the supplies are dwindling. This is rapidly turning into a bad party. As host, the logical thing to do is to bar the door and not let anyone else in.

Traditional development patterns were a good party. While each neighborhood began modestly as a collection of small investments, each new arrival simply made things better. Not only did new construction improve underlying land values in a virtuous cycle of growth, stagnation, and renewal, but it improved the capacity of the neighborhood to take collective action.

Get enough people and you could start a bucket brigade. Add some more and you can afford to put in a water line. Even more and those gravel roads could be paved. Keep growing and you could staff a police department or a library. In a good party, private growth provides collective benefits.

Modern development, where the public sector leads and everything is built to a finished state, is a bad party. When someone buys that new house on the cul-de-sac, they don't want more development around them. To the contrary; new development merely means more traffic, more people using the park, more taxes.

In our bad development party, there is no reason to expect new growth in a neighborhood to provide any real benefit to that neighborhood. There is already a paved street. The water and sewer system are already installed. The park is built, the fire station staffed, and the library is open. What benefit is there to me for adding a bunch of new people to my cul-de-sac? Little to none.

When we build all at once to a finished state, when the public sector takes the risk and leads the way on new development, then what is built is designed to decline. It lacks adaptability, both in its design and in the cultural expectations of its occupants. We've transformed our human habitat into a bad party.

Earlier in this chapter, I described the value of taking small steps in the dark and the dangers of large leaps. There is an important variation on that story that applies to situations where many people are leaping simultaneously.

If we collectively don't care how many broken noses there are so long as we gain knowledge of where the door is, just have a bunch of people take huge leaps in different directions. If nine out of ten people come to ruin breaking their noses crashing into things, but one discovers the exit, then the desired knowledge has been gained. Subsequent leapers can confidently follow that one successful person through the dark to the door.

In our post–World War II affluence, we've developed a broad cultural willingness to have our cities take large, repeated leaps in the dark. We've simultaneously increased our aversion to broken noses. We want great risk and rapid advancement, but we don't want any sacrifice or pain. Unfortunately, that's not how complex systems work.

Note

1. Census.gov, https://www.census.gov/const/C25Ann/sftotalmedavgsqft.pdf.

3

An Infinite Game

Should cities seek to run a profit?

I routinely ask audiences this question, and the feedback I get generally falls somewhere between contempt and disgust. People say, *of course, local governments should not run a profit.* The very suggestion is offensive for many who believe that local government is about serving people. It is the way we work together to do things – services that a marketplace focusing on profit just can't accomplish.

Even though it is wrong, I understand this reaction. When the term *profit* is used, it is not difficult to envision the corporate CEO whose supposed duty to shareholders is to maximize profit, particularly near-term profit, regardless of the costs to others. That doesn't seem like the kind of mentality we want directing the actions of local government.

Yet, profit is merely an accounting term that describes a condition where revenues exceed expenses. On a year-to-year basis, an orphanage must run a profit. A shelter for abandoned pets must run a profit. A palliative care clinic must have revenues that exceed expenses or, regardless of the public good that they perform in their mission, they will cease to exist.

Cities are not exempted from having to run a profit. Although a city can sometimes run a deficit year-to-year, over the long term, a local government must have revenues that exceed expenses. The only difference in this regard between a local government and a business, orphanage, or pet shelter is that, if the city fails to run a profit, it doesn't cease to exist.

An insolvent city will linger on, performing its functions poorly, failing to serve – and in some instances, doing harm to – the people that form the community it governs. For cities to function properly, running a profit is essential. For those involved in local government, it must be a functional obsession.

An Infinite Game

A baseball game has a beginning and an end. There are rules for keeping score and a way to determine the winner once the game has concluded. The pursuit of victory, within the constraints of the rules, will lead to many different strategies – approaches that can be tested, refined, and adapted over multiple games.

Now, imagine a baseball game that didn't end, one that went on inning after inning, forever. Pitchers took the mound, batters came up to the plate, runs were scored and outs were made, but the game never concluded. The rules of how to play the game might be the same, but without a condition for finality, the game would be played much differently. The objective would shift from scoring the most runs to outlasting your opponent, from run production to lineup stability.

An infinite game wouldn't be played to win, but to survive. In such a game, the day-to-day play would become ultra-conservative. Not only would players consider opportunities to score; they would also heavily weigh the risk involved with each move. A chance for a big gain would not be worth it if it entailed even a moderate chance of failure.

In fact, keeping score as a way to measure one team against the other would become meaningless, as eventually would the scoring of runs. Even if the rules of how to play remained the same, the game would fundamentally change. Instead of players focusing on competition with a rival, the focus would shift to supporting the players on one's own team. Without any chance of final victory, new forms of cooperation with the other team – sometimes called the "unwritten rules of the game" – would also emerge. Nobody would slide hard into a base, throw a fastball high and tight, or run over the catcher on a play at the plate. In an infinite game, these things wouldn't be accepted.

Now, imagine that individual baseball players were compensated based on how well they performed within the infinite game. Players who scored a lot of runs were paid more than those who didn't. This would create a personal incentive that runs counter to the communal instinct brought about by the infinite nature of the game.

It's not hard to see how this could create tension. The communal dynamic of the team in an infinite game would be threatened by a player who could gain individually in the short-term at the expense of the team's long-term stability. Different ways to harmonize these competing objectives would evolve as the game progressed.

Players might work cooperatively to make sure everyone gets a chance at a bump in pay. They might enact sanctions, like shunning players who act selfishly or benching players who refuse to play in the team's best interest. They may give added prestige to players who act selflessly. In an infinite game, a culture would evolve reflecting the unique dynamics of each team.

This is all difficult to wrap our minds around because baseball, as we experience it, is a finite game. It has a beginning and an end, a way to score, and a clear measurement of victory. We can watch an entire game, and identify the victor, in an afternoon.

While over a longer timescale, this is the same way we experience private-sector businesses. We get excited when a new coffee shop opens up the street. When it serves us well, the owner makes a profit. Other coffee shop owners take note, adapt to the demands of patrons, and there is healthy competition. Over time, weaker competitors will leave the market – they will lose the game – and new competitors will emerge.

A coffee shop owner who is too conservative – serves only one form of dark coffee – will fail and go away. A coffee shop owner who takes too many risks – introduces line after line of expensive chilled drinks – will eventually make a serious mistake, fail, and go away. Run this competition out in time, and all competitors converge on the same outcome: They will all eventually fail and be replaced by new upstarts. Running a business in the private sector is not an infinite game.

This makes both the baseball game and the private sector business very different than a city. The development of a city is an infinite game. A successful city does not have an end date. There might be some scorekeeping along the way, but there is no path to ultimate victory. As uninspiring as it may be, the primary goal of a city must be to endure.

This makes the development of a city an inherently conservative undertaking, one where risk-taking should be embraced only to the extent that it adds to the overall stability of the community.

There is a natural tension in successful cities between the collective goal of the community to endure and the individual goals of those within it. The individuals, families, businesses, and other organizations that make up the city are playing finite games. They are out to win, however they measure that. Their goal is not to endure indefinitely. In this way, the short-term incentives of individual players conflict with the long-term objective of the community.

The community must operate at a profit; its wealth must exceed its liabilities and its revenues must consistently exceed its expenses. There are many other objectives that can be pursued within that framework, but survival is a prerequisite for all of them. In a sense, it is the primary rule. If the city is to endure, the individual competing objectives must be harmonized so they do not undermine the community.

As previously noted, traditional cities – the human habitat evolved over thousands of years through trial and error experimentation – achieved this balance in novel ways. These mechanisms were quite often constraining and harsh, as all evolved systems can be. I'm not attempting to discount that reality. Yet, they fulfilled the prerequisite: They endured. Places that were not successful in harmonizing competing interests went away, their failures adding to a reservoir of cultural wisdom on how to build great places.

Our modern experiment in city-building has drained this reservoir, sacrificing the stability of the community for the short-term objectives of finite players. In many cases, the inspiration for change was virtuous, but even good intentions don't exempt communities from having to operate at a profit.

Revenues and Expenses

Nearly all local governments generate their revenue from the wealth of the community. Cities levy taxes and fees to tap into this wealth. It is a common historical practice to tax property or land. Sales taxes or transaction fees are commonly used to extract wealth when money changes hands. Local governments also charge fees for services.

Public infrastructure is a communal investment to accelerate wealth creation within a community. When, in the infinite game of city-building, the public assumes the obligation of maintaining a piece of infrastructure, the wealth that results from that investment must not only eternally cover the maintenance costs of that infrastructure; it must also contribute to the overall prosperity of the community.

If the city spends $1 million repairing a street, it's not sufficient for the tax base served by that street to only produce $1 million of revenue over the life of that street. If that's all that results, then why bother? The public doesn't build infrastructure just to have infrastructure.

For that $1 million street to be a public investment that benefits the community, it needs to do more than merely support the tax base needed to cover its own maintenance. It also needs to induce enough wealth to pay for the police and fire protection the development requires. The homes and businesses along that street must produce enough tax revenue to pay for their share of maintaining the parks, keeping the street lights on, operating the library, and running elections.

And where they do not, other places in the system must produce excess wealth to make up the difference. It's one thing to widen that two-lane street to a four-lane to handle increased traffic flow, but if that increase in traffic doesn't generate more wealth – if it is merely the same people driving more, just with fewer delays – then those added lanes are more of a luxury item than an investment.

From a financial standpoint, for something to be an investment, it must pay a return. For a city to endure, its wealth must be sufficient to maintain its basic infrastructure, provide for all the required services that accompany that development, and pay for the nonreturning luxury items we desire. Those are serious, but very real, constraints.

This makes it sound like we can't have anything nice. That is true only if we ignore the return on investment, if we don't bother to ensure that the wealth we are creating generates sufficient revenues to cover our expenses. If we obsess about running a profit, we can have things that are very nice. Quite spectacular, in fact.

Consider a standard city hall building from the early 1900s. This is one of those required investments, something that is necessary to support the community. That didn't keep our ancestors from constructing city halls that were spectacular works of art. Poor and struggling communities across North America had city halls with Roman columns, vaulted domes, and marble staircases.

They didn't do this because they were vain. They didn't do it to exalt government employees or local elected officials. And they didn't do it because they had excess cash laying around. They built them this way because that is how you squeeze a return out of an otherwise nonreturning investment.

When a local government builds a new city hall today, our cultural consensus is to look for the cheapest land available that can accommodate a nondescript office building surrounding by parking lots. The building serves a one-dimensional function and so the objective is to lower the public's cost as far as possible. Sometimes we'll squeeze in a little bit of public art so the person getting their dog license can be exposed to an abstract painting, but the art is a luxury, not a wealth-creation strategy.

Our ancestors did the opposite. They put city hall in a prime location, often at the terminating point of a major street to make it more visible. They used Classical architecture – strong, vertical symmetry – as a billboard to advertise the enduring stability of the community. They filled the building and the area around it with statues and icons to promote cooperative behavior among citizens, from the Ten Commandments to a statue of a local dignitary, someone who had done something noble, perhaps sharing their wealth for the construction of the building.

By constructing city hall in the manner in which they did, they took a building that would otherwise be merely functional and transformed it into something that radiated wealth to the community. Others would now want to be in proximity to this great building, either next door or along the street that it

terminated. Land values would go up, the virtuous cycle of redevelopment continued.

This same approach can be observed with parks, schools,
libraries, and even street lighting. These were luxury goods –
they were not essential, but they did improve the quality of life
– yet they were generally built in a manner that went beyond
utilitarian and into wealth creation.

When they were built, that is. Cities never started with
the ornate city hall. That came later, after there was sufficient
wealth to justify it. In the decades preceding its construction,
public business might be conducted in the local saloon or the
back office of the school building. That's because the city hall
building is not an investment; for the community, it's a luxury.

Our common language describes many things as "investments" that don't have a measurable return. We invest time with
our families because it pays off in happiness. We invest money
in parks because they improve our quality of life. We invest in
education because it improves society. I value all these forms of
investment, but in the context of the collective undertaking of
running a city, these luxuries – which add so much value to our
lives – are the reason we must be disciplined about the return on
our financial investments.

In the infinite game of city-building, a financial investment
must pay a return. If it doesn't pay a return, it should be looked
at as a luxury. The wealthier a city becomes, the more luxuries
it can support. Cities can be particularly successful with luxuries
when they leverage their placement, design, and functionality to
accelerate the community's wealth.

Infrastructure Not as a Means, but as an End

I ran my own planning and engineering firm for more than a
decade. One of our clients was the city of Pequot Lakes, Minnesota. During the time I worked with them, Pequot Lakes

struggled with a decision on whether to widen a two-lane high-way that ran through the middle of town into a four-lane or construct a four-lane bypass around the entire core of the city. It was a deeply contentious conversation.

One of the things we did to help public officials reach a decision was to study the financial costs and benefits of each alternative. For each alternative, the city was going to have infrastructure costs of its own as part of the project. The city engineer had recommended variants on each of these to allow the city to either (a) do the minimal amount necessary, (b) make timely maintenance investments to replace old infrastructure, or (c) make additional investments to facilitate future development within the city limits. We asked the engineer to provide costs for each of these variations.

We also brought in an outside financial expert named Jon Commers from the firm Donjek[1] to determine the revenue potential with each of these scenarios. We asked Jon to examine the city's tax base and make projections for how much private wealth could be created based on each level of public investment. Then, given the city's tax rates, we asked Jon to tell us what that would mean for the public's return on investment. In net present value, how many dollars did the city expect to get back for each dollar it spent?

Going into the meeting where the results were shared, I had a pretty good sense of how things would go. After all, I had been advising cities on making multimillion-dollar infrastructure investments for some time and felt confident in my approach. I agreed with the city's engineer's recommendation to, essentially, go big or go home: make the larger strategic investments now and the city was going to have financial rewards in the future. It was option (c), with my hunch that the bypass would prove to be the most profitable.

I was at a total loss when the results were presented. This was before the 2008 housing crisis, thus optimism was built into these calculations. Even so, for every dollar potentially to be invested by Pequot Lakes, here is the projected return on investment in each scenario:

Through Town Alternative

   (a) Required Improvements: –$7.34
   (b) Required and Maintenance Improvements: –$34.32
   (c) Required, Maintenance, and Growth Improvements: –$46.63

Bypass Alternative

   (a) Required Improvements: +$1.43
   (b) Required and Maintenance Improvements: –$3.11
   (c) Required, Maintenance, and Growth Improvements: –$12.62

    The city of Pequot Lakes was expected to lose money on all but one scenario. The only scenario they would not lose money on was one where the state highway bypassed the community with the city doing next to nothing, a giving up strategy that felt a lot like losing. In the alternative I personally supported, the city would spend $1.5 million and expect to see revenues, over the life of the improvements, of just $121,000. This just didn't seem possible.

    Yet, I had the numbers in front of me. I had set up the study asking a question I assumed I knew the answer to, yet had never seen calculated by any engineer, planner, or economic development advisor before. It was disorienting to look at the data in this way.

    I became obsessed with understanding municipal finance. As an engineer, I knew how to calculate the cost of infrastructure. It had never occurred to me that I could calculate the associated revenues. I never needed to. Nobody had ever bothered to ask!

    I started to look at projects I knew well. The first was my own home. At the time, my wife and I lived in a single-family house on a cul-de-sac with a paved road. When the road was surfaced, the city paid half the cost while my neighbors and I paid the other half. I ran the numbers; it would take 37 years of my neighbors and I paying taxes for the city to merely recoup the cost they had initially put into building the road.

That was longer than the road was going to last. It was a dead-end road; we were the only ones who used it. If my taxes weren't even enough to cover the initial construction costs, who was ever going to pay to fix it? Again, how was this possible?

There was another city I was working with that had just completed a contentious road reconstruction project. It was more intensely developed than my cul-de-sac – smaller lots, higher density – and the properties were far more valuable. This was another dead-end scenario where the street existed solely to serve the property owners living there. If there were no homes, there would be no need for the street. There was not going to be any future building or extensions to other properties that could be developed. This was it; it was built out.

Based on the taxes the city received from the property owners on the street, it was going to take that city 79 years to recoup the money they had spent on a simple maintenance project. This was bizarre! It was basic maintenance, after all. I calculated how much taxes would need to go up if the city attempted to recoup enough money from these property owners to pay for the ongoing maintenance of their own street. It would require an immediate 46% increase in taxes, with annual increases of 3% over the rate of construction cost inflation for each of the next 25 years.

There was no way that was going to happen, but that was only a small part of the problem. I assumed in my calculations that every penny of taxes the home owners paid for street maintenance was spent on *their own* street. I knew that was absurd. That little local street was the cheapest bit of transportation infrastructure in the city. I was ignoring any contribution those property owners might be expected to make for all the collector and arterial roads that these homeowners depended on, investments that were far costlier to sustain. Where was that money coming from?

I subsequently modeled dozens of residential developments – urban, suburban, exurban, and rural – and I could not find one that came close to covering its own basic expenses, let alone the collector roads, traffic signals, bridges, interchanges, and other communal expenses those revenue streams were expected to support. Not a single one.

I shifted my efforts to commercial developments and found the same long-term insolvency. A business park I had worked on as a young engineer was, after more than a decade of development, nearly built-out; almost every lot was occupied by a building. The city felt it was so successful that they wanted to build another in the same configuration, on property adjacent to the existing site.

I assumed the new business park would cost the same, and yield the same tax base, as the existing one. If that were the case, the revenue coming in wouldn't even cover the interest on a bond the city would take out to pay the up-front costs.

In examining the existing park, I found a number of sites that were not taxpaying, things like churches and public maintenance buildings. There were many more that received significant tax subsidies as an enticement to move into the park. The only way I could make the numbers cash flow for the proposed development was to assume that every lot would be developed within a year of the new business park opening, that every new building would be occupied by a taxpaying entity, that no property would be subsidized, and that all of the revenue would go to retiring the project debt.

If this were to occur, it would still take 29 years for the debt to be retired. That's nearly three decades where taxes would need to go up for everyone else in the community to cover the snow plowing, crack sealing, police and fire protection, and all the other services needed within the new business park. And that's with a wildly optimistic scenario; anything remotely realistic didn't even cover its own debt payments.

I started to share this information with professional colleagues and public officials in the cities I worked with. In a sense, I didn't believe my own data. I was convinced there was something I was missing, and my professional colleagues had plenty of theories.

The dominant critique was that I was not properly considering the value of job creation. I found this frustratingly absurd. Of course, job creation has a benefit and our cities will not last long without jobs, but where in the municipal revenue stream does a job show up? While some cities have an income tax, the ones I was looking at did not. Without a way to monetize the value of a job, there was no functional difference between a municipal investment that created a job and one that did not.

We're conditioned to think otherwise, so let me explain this using an extreme analogy. Pretend there are two cities. The first we'll call Housing City and the second we'll call Job City. A thousand people live in Housing City. They each have their own home. Every day, those thousand people travel to Job City where they work in a call center located in a tent in the middle of a field.

In a system where municipalities are funded by a property or land tax, Housing City has no jobs, yet it has a thousand homes it can tax and receive revenue from. Job City has at least a thousand jobs, yet the tax base of the tent in the field is relatively tiny by comparison. Regardless of how much those jobs pay, Job City will not receive any revenue from their existence. The public officials and professional staff in Job City might be happy to have so much employment but, without the tax base from the housing, they are not going to have much revenue to pay their bills.

The same can often be said of sales tax. In Minnesota, we do have sales tax, but – except in some limited and special circumstances – the money goes to the state, not the local government. A city can have a massive collection of big-box stores and car dealerships, sucking transactions out of all the surrounding region into its own commercial strip, yet without a sales tax, those transactions don't show up in the municipality's revenue stream.

While I hadn't at the time, I've now had the opportunity to look at systems where sales and income taxes are collected by local governments. While there are some modest differences, the overall effect is the same as with property tax systems; the revenue streams generated are insufficient to meet base infrastructure liabilities.

Beyond job creation and sales taxes, the critiques I was getting from professional colleagues fell along the lines of "people want it," as if that was some kind of holy blessing. People wanted cul-de-sacs, spread-out development patterns, drive-through restaurants, and lots of parking. And because people wanted it, they will find a way to pay for it, and that was all the justification needed to get going.

Coming from professionals who were compensated for building all this stuff, that attitude seemed stunningly self-serving. Don't we have an obligation to make sure that what we built could plausibly be sustained by future generations? It was Upton Sinclair who said, "It is difficult to get a man to understand something when his salary depends on his not understanding it." With a few notable exceptions, I found Sinclair's observation maddeningly insightful.

For me, the evidence was pointing to a conclusion I found difficult to believe, yet impossible to ignore: The more our cities build, the poorer they become.

The Municipal Ponzi Scheme

When local governments need professional assistance, they often issue what is called a request for proposal (RFP). Consultants like myself respond to the RFP and, if successful, there is an interview. I've done many such interviews, answering questions from city staff as well as elected and appointed public officials.

One might expect such interviews to delve into the competence of the professional seeking to provide services, but I was never asked about my engineering or planning expertise. There were only two questions public officials were interested in, and they are closely related:

1. How good are you at getting funding for a project?
2. How good are you at working with the public to sell the project we want to do?

These questions would be asked in different ways, but it was always the same. For example, funding might involve a federal grant application or a routine property assessment. Even though this had nothing to do with the engineering of the project, I was expected to show confidence in being able to fill out the right forms, meet with the right people, and score highly in whatever process the city wanted to pursue.

When it came to the public, we would be briefed on the (perceived) uninformed malcontents who were sure to oppose the project, or the sensitive cultural concern unique to the community, and queried as to how skilled we were in making these people feel listened to – or at least provide the outward appearances of such – while still shepherding the project through.

In the end, it was all about growth. The common denominator was that every city wanted to grow; my job was to help them do that. It was clear how this benefitted me – I got paid to do the project – but what wasn't clear to me, now that I had mounds of data, was why cities wanted to grow if it was going to make them poorer.

I understood that a growing city *looked* good. That new street without a crack or weed looks like prosperity compared to the old, rutted road. That new house in the new subdivision has an aura of prosperity that is lacking in older neighborhoods. Is our obsession with growth merely superficial? That felt incomplete.

I also understood the allure of ribbon cuttings and grand openings, the ability to convey a sense of progress by an act of political theater. There is something viscerally satisfying in blaming the morally compromised politician who can bring home the pork-barrel project. Yet, this answer also felt incomplete. I worked with a lot of politicians, and a lot of other professionals, and while few would pass up an opportunity for self-congratulation, I never got the sense that was the motivation. There is something more.

In a macroeconomic sense, I'm going to explain that "more" in greater detail in the next two chapters. For local governments, it actually becomes quite simple: New growth provides local governments an opportunity to receive additional cash in the short term in exchange for taking on unpayable, long-term liabilities. The mechanism is stunningly simple.

Consider the ideal scenario: a developer who comes to town and is willing to invest their own money to bring a project to fruition. This developer seeks no public assistance or subsidy. They are willing to follow all the rules and regulations of the community. They will, at their own expense, build all the residential homes and commercial buildings within the development. They will install and pay for, to the municipality's standards, all the required roads, streets, curbs, sidewalks, pipes, pumps, valves, and meters.

The only thing the developer asks for making this investment in the community is that the local government – steward of the public balance sheet – agree to take over the long-term responsibility to service and maintain this new development. All the city must do is provide police and fire protection, maintenance the of the infrastructure, and the other general services provided to all residents and businesses within the city.

I have never encountered a local government that wouldn't immediately accept such an offer. In fact, in many places it would be illegal not to, assuming all the local standards were met. Generally, developers ask for concessions or subsidies making the deal worse than what I'm presenting, but stick with this ideal scenario and follow the cash flow over time.

In the first year after the new development is built, everything is brand new. The streets, sidewalks, and pipes don't need any maintenance at all. Revenue from the new development pours into the city coffers. Some of it is spent on public safety, some on parks, some on running city hall, and some is spent on fixing and maintaining infrastructure in other parts of the city.

Pretend that maintenance money is sequestered. Instead of having it go to fix the street in front of the mayor's house on the other side of town, it's set aside and saved for the day when the city must go out and make good on the promise they made to fix and maintain the street in the new development.

Every year, more tax revenue is added to the fund. For decades, nothing is being spent. A 5-year-old road isn't costing the city anything. A 10-year-old sidewalk presents no immediate expense. A 15-year-old pipe is just fine sitting there in the ground. It's only when we get a generation out, when the city is expected to go out and perform maintenance or rehabilitation of that infrastructure, that the insolvency is revealed. It's at this point that cash flow runs far into the negative (Figure 3.1).

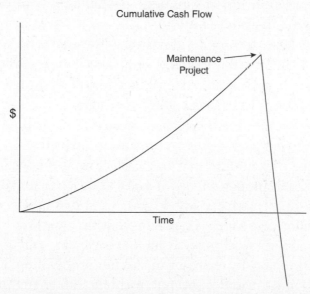

Figure 3.1 Municipal Cash Flow over One Life Cycle for a Single Development

Cities don't sequester money in this way. Some are prohibited from doing so and, even if they were allowed, it's very questionable whether society would want local governments hoarding capital. Nonetheless, what this demonstrates is that, for two or three decades, the city was receiving cash from this new development that they were free to spend elsewhere, despite the looming, and easily predictable, maintenance obligation.

For cities in need of cash, new growth provides it. In the pattern of development we're experimenting with today – one that is government-led, spread out, and mostly homogenous across the entire continent – new growth gives a local government decades of free cash flow. That makes it easy to understand the natural reaction of city leadership, as well as American society in general, when those liabilities come due and the insolvency starts to bite: pursue more growth.

The general attitude is to return to what worked, or what appeared to work in the memories of those assembled to evaluate such things. When the city was growing, things looked successful and there was excess cash available; let's get things growing again. That's a powerful argument, particularly because it's not without some basis in reality.

Go back to the model developer, the one who offered to build everything if the city will only maintain it. Pretend that this developer returns a couple years after the first project with a similar proposal. Then every other year from that point forward, a developer comes forth offering likewise. This is the ideal scenario for any city: nice, steady, continuous growth.

Instead of spending that free cash flow, if the local government took that money and set it aside in order to make good on the promises they are making, Figure 3.2 shows how tax revenue would accumulate for that same 25-year time period.

There is a lot of growth happening here, and so a lot of cash accumulates. In terms of infrastructure maintenance, each development contributes revenue without adding any immediate

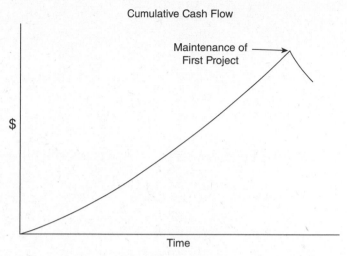

Figure 3.2 Municipal Cash Flow over One Life Cycle for Multiple Developments in Sequence

expense. With all the growth happening, revenues accelerate upward. After two decades of saving, this local government is sitting on a huge pile of cash.

And in year 25, when the maintenance liability for that first development comes due, the city is required to draw on the savings to make good on the promise, but it's not a big deal. The money is there because of all the growth.

The growth creates an illusion of wealth, a broad, cultural misperception that the growing community is become stronger and more prosperous. Instead, with each new development, they become increasingly more insolvent. When a city loses money over the long term on every project it does, it doesn't make up the difference in volume. The more time that passes, the more downward pressure there is on the budget (Figure 3.3). Continuing to grow in this pattern only buys time. And time only makes the urgency to grow even greater.

Local governments now exist in a time defined by their past promises. The liabilities from decades of unproductive development are coming due. All those miles of roads, all those pipes

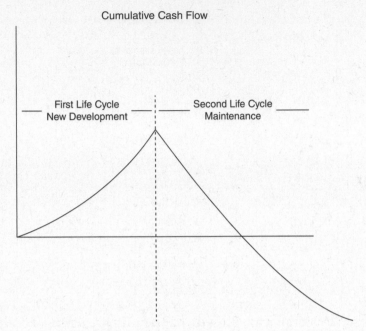

Cumulative Cash Flow

First Life Cycle
New Development

Second Life Cycle
Maintenance

Figure 3.3 Municipal Cash Flow over Two Life Cycles for Multiple Developments in Sequence

and pumps, all the bridges, the storage systems, the buildings . . . all of it must now be maintained. Our cities are so spread out and denuded, the wealth is not there to pay for it all.

The growth that was supported by all this public investment did not result in enough prosperity to maintain all that was built. And if our cities could somehow come up with the money – for example, if the federal government tried to bail out every city struggling to maintain cul-de-sacs, frontage roads, and water loops – they would only be doubling down on a wealth-destroying series of public investments, buying time in a race to the financial bottom.

Public pensions are frequently cited as the municipal crisis of our time, but even they are merely symptoms of incorrect assumptions about our development pattern. When cities ran short of cash yet needed to negotiate contracts with their employees' unions, it was straightforward for everyone to forgo salary today for an increased pension tomorrow. The city would invest those savings in growth, which, everyone assumed, would pay off, making those pensions easily affordable. Tragically, they were wrong.

And public officials did not pocket the money they were supposed to send to the pension funds, like some greedy corporate executive. They spent it running the city, often based on the recommendations of the staff they were shortchanging. Despite the frequent caricature, these are not bad or incompetent people. While we can all be self-serving at times, I've yet to meet an elected official that wasn't sincerely doing what they thought best. Sure, they might strategically reduce a pension payment, but if they were investing in growing the city, there was a broad cultural consensus that it would work out better for everyone.

Local elected officials, and the professional staffs that serve them, all pretty much bought into the prosperity narrative around our growth-based development pattern. In that, they are simply human, all too human.

The Illusion of Wealth

We should all recognize our own behavior in that last chart. It's the reason why people smoke. It's why many of us struggle with dieting. Why we'll sit in front of the television instead of going for a walk. In our minds we understand lung cancer, diabetes, and heart disease, but those are very distant threats. And the pleasure from smoking, sugar, and inactivity are very real and very now.

Humans have a propensity to highly value pleasurable feedback today and to deeply discount potential negative consequences in the distant future. Psychologists call this effect temporal discounting. While it is not difficult to imagine why wiring humans for such opportunistic behavior would provide an evolutionary advantage, it's also clear why, in a world lacking the constraints that humans evolved with, this could now prove problematic.

Hundreds of thousands of years ago, it would have been folly for a human to pass on a meal. Being opportunistic was a survival strategy. Most modern humans, especially in the United States, have continuous and predictable access to food. Restraint has become an imperative. Yet, is it simply a matter of applying modern willpower to overcoming evolutionary shortcomings?

In his book *The World Until Yesterday: What We Can Learn from Traditional Societies*, Jared Diamond describes the perfect physiology for a hunter-gatherer living in a traditional society. Due to food insecurity, they would have been able to gorge themselves whenever food was available. Their bodies would have converted as many of those calories as possible to body fat. They would then burn that stored energy as slowly as possible, giving themselves that maximum chance for survival between meals.

> Under these traditional conditions of starve-and-gorge existence, those individuals with a thrifty genotype would be at an advantage, because they could store more fat in surplus times, burn fewer calories in spartan times, and hence better survive starvation. To most humans until recently, our modern Western fear of obesity and our diet clinics would have seemed ludicrous, as the exact reverse of traditional good sense.
>
> The genes that today predispose us to diabetes may formerly have helped us to survive famine. Similarly, our "taste" for sweet or fatty foods, like our taste for salt, predisposes us to diabetes and hypertension now that those tastes can be satisfied so easily, but formerly guided us to seek valuable rare nutrients.
>
> Note . . . the evolutionary irony. Those of us whose ancestors best survived starvation on Africa's savannahs tens of thousands of years ago are now the ones at highest risk of dying from diabetes linked to food abundance.[2]

Today, Pacific Islanders, whose forced adjustment to the modern diet occurred over years instead of generations, suffer from incredible rates of obesity and diabetes. The World Health Organization has reported that within many Pacific Island countries, more than 50%, and sometimes up to 90%, of the population is overweight. Obesity rates range from 30% in Figi to 80% among females in American Samoa.[3] This is not a matter of willpower but rather our shared genetic dispositions.

Diamond speculates that, before modern medicine, European populations "may have undergone an epidemic of diabetes" from suddenly having access to abundant food. Those poorly adapted to abundance would have died early, not reproducing or, where they did, leaving their children and descendants at a serious disadvantage for survival. The replacement of the starvation-hardened by those more well-adapted to a modern diet is a good explanation for why European rates of diabetes are comparatively low (10.3% for men and 9.6% for women).[4]

Complex, adaptive systems learn through destruction. It's not survival of the fittest – a phrase often misattributed to Charles Darwin – but rather, survival of the most adaptable. The fittest in one time and place may be at a fatal disadvantage in another. It's those who can survive in both that have the opportunity to flourish.

Author of *The Black Swan*, Nassim Taleb, in a 2013 speech at Loyola College titled "How to Live in a World We Don't Understand," explained how humans have reacted to abundance – to a lack of constraints – by exercising more control over their environment, repeatedly solving the immediate problem at the expense of our overall stability.

> With the enlightenment, the industrial revolution, came a greater control over our environment. So what did we get? The smoothness. We remove everything. We smooth out the economic cycles. No more up and down. It's okay until it blows up.
>
> You want to smooth out the forest fires? It's okay, but without fires, the forest blows up. You want to make people comfortable? Okay, but their bone density goes down.[5]

This is a central theme for both Taleb and Diamond, the two modern authors who have most influenced my thinking on these subjects. With constraints removed, surrounded by abundance, we humans are hardwired to address the immediate problem in front of us, and to overlook, or dramatically discount, the long-term consequences of that action.

When it comes to the traditional city, there was no lack of problems to address. Harmonizing all those competing interests created habitats that may have been optimized for humans, but optimized is different than optimal. I'm not criticizing the people who believed they could do better, or the people who empowered them to do so. I believe we would all have acted in the same way in that situation.

Yet, like the human evolved on a starvation-diet finding themselves in a modern society with abundant food, our habitats are now radically different than they were. They are bloated, poorly adapted, and fragile. This experiment – conducted on a continental scale – is proving to be financially ruinous. Acquiring the cash that comes with immediate growth in exchange for enormous long-term obligations is a great way to solve today's problems, but a terrible survival strategy.

For many cities, even those that are still growing, the illusion of wealth is fading. We are now 70 years into this experiment and we find ourselves with large amounts of debt while facing unpayable levels of obligations. This isn't a matter of raising taxes or cutting services to make things balance out. It is coming down to a decision more akin to triage.

Which road do we fix and which do we let fall apart? Which pipe do we repair and which one do we walk away from? Which neighborhood do we save and which do we write off?

For cities who have arrived at this point, there are no good answers. The conversation, once broached, always seems to circle around to the American case study: Detroit.

Understanding Detroit

I've traveled to hundreds of cities to speak with people about Strong Towns and, when the subject of Detroit comes up, the conversation nearly always goes the same. If the person I am speaking with is on the left of the political spectrum, they have a narrative of what has happened in Detroit that is internally coherent with their worldview. *It was greedy corporations or Wall Street swindlers or a lack of social empathy for the underprivileged.*

If the person I am speaking with is on the right of the political spectrum, they have a narrative on Detroit that is also internally coherent with their worldview. *It was inept government or the destruction of the family or crony corruption.*

While internally coherent, these narratives have no overlap, except for one point: We are not Detroit. Nearly everyone I have spoken with sees Detroit as a kind of anomaly, some strange place unlike any other in America, and certainly unlike the place they live. *We are not Detroit and what happened there could never happen here.*

My narrative of Detroit is different. It starts with acknowledging that, prior to the Great Depression, Detroit was one of the greatest cities in the world. It was certainly one of the richest. Even today, it is breathtaking to visit places like the Detroit Opera House, opened in 1922, and realize that it would be stunning even in the wealthiest of European capitals. The amazing buildings still there today speak to Detroit's once tremendous wealth and prestige.

In the early 1900s, as Detroit was on its way to becoming the Motor City, it became the first major city in the world to start experimenting with what would become the American development pattern. They were the first to create automobile suburbs. The first to experience people commuting into the city by day, returning home by car at night. They were the first to run major roadways through their neighborhoods. They were the first to tear down buildings and turn over large portions of the public realm for parking.

They were the first to transform the human habitat into what we recognize today as the modern North American city. And when society reached the Great Depression and cities around the country started to experience major distress, losing jobs and dislocating populations, there was a cluster of places centered on Detroit that fared comparatively well. So much so that, by the end of World War II, it was very clear to a victorious nation what needed to happen if we wanted to keep from sliding back into economic depression: We all needed to copy the success of Detroit. That is what we did.

When you take a prosperous and stable city, spread it out at tremendous cost over an enormous area, denuding and bisecting the original fabric as part of the transition, then saddle it with decades of liabilities, you end up with Detroit. Like all bankruptcies, it happened slowly and then all at once.

Detroit is not some strange anomaly. It's just early. It's just a couple of decades ahead of everyplace else.

Notes

1. Disclosure: Jon and I would become good friends after this project. It was his idea to form a nonprofit named Strong Towns to explore the startling ideas we started to uncover in Pequot Lakes.
2. Jared Diamond, *The World Until Yesterday: What We Can Learn from Traditional Societies* (New York: Penguin Books, 2012).
3. http://www.who.int/bulletin/volumes/88/7/10-010710/en/.
4. http://www.euro.who.int/en/health-topics/noncommunicable-diseases/diabetes/data-and-statistics.
5. https://www.youtube.com/watch?time_continue=948&v=iEnmjMgP_Jo.

4

The Infrastructure Cult

The point is that perfectly standard, mainstream economics makes a powerful case for much more infrastructure spending. And this needs to be said often.[1]
—Paul Krugman, Nobel Prize–winning economist

The case for a substantially increased programme of public infrastructure is undeniable.[2]
—Lawrence Summers, former U.S. Secretary of the Treasury

This is America. We've always had the best infrastructure.[3]
—Barack Obama, 44th president of the United States

We need once and for all to have a very big infrastructure program.[4]
—Hillary Clinton, 2016 Democratic presidential candidate

Infrastructure – we're going to start spending on infrastructure big. Not like we have a choice.[5]
—Donald Trump, President of the United States

The last thing that our cities need is more infrastructure. Yet, at a time noted for political polarization and bitter divisiveness, the only thing our politicians, professionals, and the working class all seem to agree on is spending for infrastructure. Support for infrastructure investments continually poll higher than any other policy item under consideration.[6] Voters have even demonstrated a willingness to accept modest tax increases if the money is dedicated to infrastructure.

The cultural narrative for infrastructure spending is a pretty easy sell: Building infrastructure creates jobs as well as other development opportunities. It will shorten commutes and keep the environment cleaner. And just look around at all the crumbling infrastructure in the United States; infrastructure investment is seen as a bipartisan no-brainer.

We can somewhat let the broader American public off the hook. It's not their job to manage our infrastructure; they don't have the spreadsheets of the cash flow, a tally of the cost of maintenance, the present condition of these systems, and all the other blinking red lights on the dashboard of America's cities. Polls have shown that Americans want infrastructure maintained more than they want these systems expanded.[7]

What should baffle us, however, is how professionals and decision-makers are so possessed by faith in infrastructure spending. Cities with a mind-boggling backlog of unfunded road maintenance routinely go out and build new roads. Places with pipes crumbling and pumps failing from lack of maintenance give incentives to developers to build more pipes and pumps for the public to maintain. How could they be so myopic, so lacking in introspection, to intentionally add more water to their already capsizing ship?

It's easy to assume that those involved in these decisions are acting in their own self-interest, but this is more than just ribbon cuttings or kickbacks. And it's more than job security for the engineer, planners, and the other city-building professionals who do this work. I will not deny that personal benefit is a seductive reinforcement to their thinking, but the intellectual capture of the belief in building infrastructure goes much deeper.

This also can't solely be attributed to the pyramid-scheme nature of our development pattern, the cognitive discounting that prompts us to highly value the cash benefits today while ignoring the long-term financial consequences of our decisions. Even when the negative financial math on a project is easily discernible, even when the cash payout isn't there, public officials often vote – with the recommendation of their professional staff – to move ahead with infrastructure spending.

The ultimate victory of any ideology is to no longer be considered an ideology, merely truth. Our collective belief in the power of infrastructure spending is now so deeply embedded within our society that we struggle to identify it as belief, let alone systematically question it. We take it as truth, unequivocally.

A cult is a collection of people having a misplaced or excessive admiration for a person or thing. Since the end of World War II, America's leadership class has grown to be an infrastructure cult.

The American Society of Civil Engineers

The American Society of Civil Engineers (ASCE) is the most authoritative, prestigious, and oft-quoted organization on North American infrastructure spending. Their periodic report cards routinely score U.S. infrastructure at just above failing. With the enthusiastic support of contractors, developers, trade unions, and others involved in the business of construction, the ASCE regularly calls for large increases in all levels of infrastructure spending. They boldly cite the obvious benefits of more infrastructure, claims that are parroted nearly unquestioned by politicians and media outlets.

For example, in 2011, as governments everywhere were having their budgets hammered by the lingering effects of the housing crisis that began three years earlier, the ASCE published a report called *Failure to Act*,[8] an analysis of the economic impacts of infrastructure investment trends. In this report, the ASCE detailed the hundreds of billions our failing infrastructure is costing American families and businesses.

At that point, ASCE estimated that families and businesses had lost $130 billion due just from deficiencies in transportation systems. Over the next decade, an additional $430 billion would be lost by businesses and $482 billion by families, all due to our failure to make the proper investments in transportation infrastructure. Taken cumulatively, this is a loss just over $1 trillion in a decade.

To avoid this loss, and to reach what the ASCE has called "minimum tolerable conditions" on the nation's highway, bridge, and transit investments, the *Failure to Act* report indicates that an additional $220 billion must be spent annually going forward. That's $2.2 trillion in additional infrastructure spending over the coming decade.

Let me summarize what you've just read: The American Society of Civil Engineers suggests that the federal government, on behalf of the American people, spend $2.2 trillion over a decade to save those same Americans from the hardship of having distressed infrastructure, a difficulty estimated to cost just $1 trillion.

How can a prestigious organization like the American Society of Civil Engineers write something that seems so nonsensical? Spend $2.2 trillion to save $1 trillion? That's preposterous!

The answer is simple: They don't consider it nonsense. They have such a deep, cult-like belief in what they are saying – as do the organizations, politicians, and media outlets that continuously repeat these assertions – that they don't even comprehend the absurdity of their own numbers.

For example, in that same report, the following assertion was made:

> By 2040, America's deteriorating surface transportation infrastructure
> is expected to cost the nation's economy more than 400,000 jobs.[9]

This was reported in numerous news outlets exactly as presented by ASCE: 400,000 fewer jobs by 2040. Yet, the week this report came out, new jobless claims were 400,000.[10] That's 400,000 jobs lost *in a single week*! The ASCE suggests Americans make $6.6 trillion in additional transportation investments over three decades in the belief that such an investment would save the economy the distress of losing 400,000 jobs, and the same news outlets reporting on jobless claims ran ASCE's projection without questioning it.

These numbers are ridiculous on their face, but dig deeper and the ridiculousness shifts dangerously to outright offensiveness. That's because, while infrastructure spending is done with real taxpayer dollars, the costs Americans would supposedly be saving themselves from are anything but hard currency.

Real Investment, Paper Returns

When it is reported that an infrastructure investment will save $1 trillion over the next decade, most people outside city-building industries, and a scary number of them within, assume that this means 1 trillion *dollars*. As in, this infrastructure investment will result in 1 trillion dollars that can be spent on something else: education, health care, perhaps defense.

I suspect this might have been true at some point in the past, before infrastructure spending became an embedded cultural belief. It is not close to being true today. Take the example of $430 billion over a decade that the ASCE suggests will be lost by businesses due to inadequate infrastructure spending. This is not dollars lost; it is a dollar equivalent for their estimate of the value of lost time.

Here is how this works: A project is proposed to add a lane to a congested highway. The highway is carrying 100,000 cars per day. Each trip is projected to be 30 seconds quicker once the new lane is completed. Project advocates would then take those 100,000 trips, multiply that by 30 seconds of saved time per trip, and conclude that the project will save 3 million seconds – roughly 830 hours – of otherwise lost time each and every day.

That's a lot of time, especially when you realize that the median worker in the market makes $25 per hour in wage and benefits. At that rate, saving 830 hours of time is equivalent to saving $21,000 per day.

And when you factor in that there are 356 days in a year and that the added lane can be expected to last at least 50 years, all of a sudden saving each person a mere 30 seconds of time on their commute results in a total of $380 million saved. Do that calculation over thousands of different projects and it adds up to hundreds of billions of dollars. Now we're talking real money!

Or are we? When confused for actual money, this saved-time calculation becomes farcical. First and most obvious, we can't pay for the asphalt, concrete, steel, engineers, and construction workers with 30-second increments of saved time. Bondholders likewise do not transact in saved time. They all require real currency. So, if the project doesn't result in the kind of growth that generates real dollars, all that saved time isn't going to matter much.

It is also important to step back and understand what is causing the lost time the project is alleviating. It's not long-haul truckers traveling from Houston to Kansas City, from Los Angeles to Tulsa. It's commuters, the kind of people induced by transportation investments to live in the developments that, as shown in Chapter 3, are bankrupting our cities through the illusion of wealth.

And despite what engineers and economists model in their spreadsheets, commuters are humans and thus react to change in complex ways. Quicken their commute by 30 seconds, and they might sleep in half a minute more, move a mile further away from where they work, or decide to drive to the store during rush hour instead of waiting until mid-morning. Either way, it's not credible to suggest that saved time is going to result in increased worker productivity, let alone create real dollars that can be recaptured to pay for the project.

The ASCE *Failure to Act* report refers to saved time, but it also refers to reduced wear and tear. This is a method to calculate how much humans will save not having to repair their vehicles as often due to improved road conditions, again, as if humans all respond in the same way. It's also quite a one-dimensional calculation; there is no consideration given, for example, to the economic benefit from employing more mechanics, auto dealers, and car manufacturers. That's not because they are any less real but because, as is obvious by now, this math the Infrastructure Cult uses is not trying to suggest anything real. It's merely assembled as propaganda.

Building a highway? Calculate the time commuters save in transit but ignore the delays they have during construction and maintenance.

Putting in a traffic signal? Calculate the value of potential new business growth but ignore the cost of time delays for people having to sit at red lights.

Putting in a frontage road? Installing a new sewer line? Building a water tower? Calculate the value of the new Walmart, McDonalds, and Jiffy Lube but ignore the negative economic effects from closing the old Walmart, McDonalds, and Jiffy Lube up the road.

A belief in the power of infrastructure investments to generate growth and prosperity is so deeply entrenched that it has impaired rational analysis. Otherwise thoughtful people will not question ridiculous notions, such as whether spending $2.2 trillion over a decade is worth it to avoid $1 trillion in losses during that same period, because it is – in their minds – unquestionable that infrastructure investment is a positive thing.

Psychologists call the human tendency to seek out affirming data, and to ignore conflicting data, confirmation bias, but this goes much deeper. The leadership class in America holds infrastructure investments in such high regard that the overwhelming benefit from new growth is simply assumed. It's a foundational belief not open to serious examination.

Accounting for Infrastructure

The cult-like belief in the value of infrastructure is evident in the way municipalities track their own wealth. In accounting terminology, the balance sheet is a ledger that lists a city's assets and liabilities, the wealth it possesses, and the claims against that wealth.

It is relatively easy to understand why a pension promise would be considered a liability. The city agrees to pay a pension benefit in the future. The value of that promise is a dollar amount that can be calculated, based on actuarial tables of life expectancy, historic rates of return for different investment approaches, and other discernable trends. Money is collected from the employee, and some contribution made by the municipality, for the purpose of meeting this future obligation.

The amount of money the city has saved to pay pensions is an asset. The amount the city is obligated to pay out for pensions – calculated in present value – is a liability. The difference between these two is either a surplus or, more likely for pensions, a deficit. It is recorded this way on the municipality's balance sheet. To overcome a deficit, more money must be set aside and/ or a reduction in benefits is necessary. This is straightforward.

It is logical to assume that infrastructure is tracked in a similar way, especially since doing so is seemingly easier than tracking pension liabilities. A new development is built. The cash flow derived from the wealth of the tax base – the taxes from all those new homes and businesses added together – is the community's asset. The easily estimated future maintenance cost is the liability. Generating a surplus year-to-year across all these developments is how the city stays in business. Again, pretty simple.

Only, that's not how infrastructure works. The generally accepted accounting practices for municipalities counts infrastructure as an asset, not a liability. There is no accounting of the tax base or the revenue from the community's wealth; it's simply ignored. With this approach, the more roads a city has, the more pipes in the ground, the more public buildings and pumps in its inventory, the richer that city is. It's backward.

Take two cities. The first has a billion dollars of tax base on one block of street. The second has only a million dollars of tax base but has five miles of street. While the first has a plenty of wealth and not much in terms of future maintenance promises to keep, the second city would have the stronger balance sheet. That's because the second city has five miles of street as an asset instead of only one block. No matter that the billion-dollar city has 1,000 times the tax base, by the method cities use for their accounting, the million-dollar city is wealthier.

Any rationally minded person understands that the street in front of your home is not an asset for the community. It can't be picked up and sold to the neighboring town. It can't be pledged as collateral against a debt. The street is a liability, plain and simple. In the infinite game of running a city, it represents an eternal commitment to ongoing maintenance and repair.

The community's asset isn't the street in front of your home; the asset is your home. Or at least the future tax revenue related to that property. The value of your home represents wealth within the community, wealth that can be tapped to meet the promises the community makes, like maintaining roads and pipes. That cash flow can be – and frequently is – pledged as collateral by the local government when they issue bonds.

It almost feels silly to have to explain something so obvious. Yet, obvious or not, every state and local government in the United States tracks its infrastructure liabilities as if they were assets, while few bother to account for, let alone track, their real wealth. If our municipalities used accurate accounting, most of them would be insolvent.

Assuming Secondary Effects

The few times when I've heard members of the Infrastructure Cult pushed to account for infrastructure spending's return on investment, they always fall back on the assumed secondary benefits. They'll argue that infrastructure spending makes the economy more efficient, for example, asserting this as de facto truth. The claim isn't tempered by the fact that nearly every American can point to a local list of wasteful infrastructure projects, investments that cost a lot but didn't seem to amount to all that much.

Somehow building a new frontage road so the Walmart on the old frontage road can be relocated is assumed to be efficient. The same with building a new highway interchange so a few hundred homes can be built an hour away from the regional employment center. When looked at individually, the public-sector math behind most of these projects makes no sense. Yet, the true believer is comfortable assuming that, if you add up all the negative-returning infrastructure investments, the network effects from them produces a platform of economic efficiency. Not only is there no evidence to support that conclusion; it defies logic.

Another favorite secondary benefit to cite is job creation. The case here is stronger at the federal level and in states and the handful of cities with an income tax, but the financial case is still more wish than rigorous reality. If half a project cost is labor, and a fourth of those wages end up paid in taxes, and 5% of those tax revenues go toward infrastructure, then the tax revenue from temporary construction jobs are covering 0.6% of any given project. I think that's optimistically high, but even if it wasn't, there are far more cost-effective ways to create jobs.

It is true that construction workers need services themselves, so putting money in their hands has secondary benefits for the overall economy. Again, we're not capturing that revenue anywhere measurable, and so correlating spending on projects we desire with positive outcomes we observe – and ignoring any contrary data – is merely a theoretical exercise in bias confirmation. Sure, that construction worker has money in his pocket to buy a coffee and that will put someone to work, but the person or the business paying the taxes on that infrastructure – or the debt on the interest – makes economic choices, too, decisions that are ignored in these one-sided calculations.

Economists like to argue that, in times of economic hardship, if we pay someone to dig a ditch and then pay them again to fill it back in, we'll stimulate the economy in helpful ways. The case for infrastructure spending is an extension of that logic: If instead of digging and filling a ditch, we spend the money on concrete, steel, and asphalt, we're actually better off because we've built something useful.

What is obvious but not acknowledged in that narrative is that, with the ditch, we ultimately end up back where we started. No long-term liability. In contrast, when we build a road or a bridge or a mile of pipe, we're left with an eternal maintenance obligation. If the project costs more than the wealth it creates – which most of the projects we are undertaking today do – then we're just getting poorer, regardless of job creation. We'd be better off digging and filling the ditch. Or just giving people money without laundering it through an infrastructure spending program.

The time savings and wear-and-tear calculations from the ASCE report are also frequently applied to transit projects, particularly large rail projects. Transit projects are generally subjected to more financial scrutiny than highway projects, but that's still a very low bar. The most commonly cited financial benefit of transit comes from freeing up congested highways, an assumed effect never witnessed anywhere in human history.

Beyond that, transit is often cited as an investment in social equity because it is seen as a benefit for the poor. As with highway investments, there are all kinds of calculations made to show the financial benefits for the disadvantaged of having improved bus or rail service. In other words, the Infrastructure

Cult argues that it's a positive economic benefit to have a development pattern that spreads everything out as far as possible; then they argue that there's even more economic benefit to provide a marginal transportation option to the growing number of people who can't afford to live in that very expensive, spread-out development pattern. I find this incoherent.

The latest fad is to tout a project's carbon-reduction benefits as a contribution to fighting climate change. For example, with all seriousness, project supporters will make a series of intellectual contortions to calculate the amount of carbon saved on a congested freeway, under the assumption that their capacity-building project reduces the amount of stop-and-go driving. They conveniently ignore the more obvious and intuitive fact that making it easier to drive means more people will drive, and more driving means more carbon, not less.

Rather than producing a multitude of unmeasurable benefits, it is far more likely that our passion for infrastructure spending is satiating a more human instinct. Psychologists call this confirmation bias. We include in our analysis the things that make the case for what we want to do, and we ignore the things that would undermine our cause. In other words, we exhibit cult-like behavior.

Calculating secondary effects and comparing them against costs is sometimes a worthy exercise, but only for projects that have a positive, real rate of return. If the project is going to lose money, and the costs continue to compound indefinitely as maintenance cycles repeat over and over, then secondary benefits are meaningless as an accounting exercise.

A Real Return on Investment

What would it mean to break out of the Infrastructure Cult and make capital investments that had a real return on investment? First and foremost, it would require us to spend public money on infrastructure projects that covered their own costs, not only today but indefinitely into the future.

This is nearly impossible with a development pattern that forces us to build in large blocks to a finished state. Such an approach forces us to make predictions about what will happen after an infrastructure investment is made, something humans have a long track record of being poor at doing. We need to know what will be built, what the market will pay for it, that it will be maintained, that the value of the developed properties will increase at rates greater than construction inflation, and so on.

For all practical purposes, this is impossible, which is one of the reasons our ancestors built their cities incrementally. Projections are not necessary and propaganda math is irrelevant when things are built incrementally with ongoing feedback driving adaptation.

If we're going to break out of the Infrastructure Cult mentality, we would need to design our systems to respond to feedback. There is no clearer feedback on value than someone's willingness to pay for something, yet our infrastructure funding mechanisms have a large degree of separation from the user's willingness to pay for what they want.

We all pay our gas tax and expect the roads to be maintained, improved, and expanded when needed. Yet, as the ASCE has suggested – I think correctly – the gas tax comes nowhere near funding transportation to even a minimum tolerable condition. The natural response then is to raise the gas tax, but doing so reduces driving, which reduces revenue, which would require an increase in the gas tax. And so on.

And the gas tax tells us nothing about the viability of a specific project. At best, it's more of a referendum on the public's perception of the value of the overall transportation system. A more direct and actionable form of feedback would be a toll, yet, in the handful of instances where infrastructure projects have included tolls as their funding mechanism, the data suggests that humans value their time differently than Infrastructure Cult models suggest they should.

The best example is the I-65 bridge in Louisville connecting Kentucky to Indiana. The states spent $1.3 billion on a congestion-reduction project including the construction of the I-65 bridge, which is now tolled up to $4 per crossing. Not only is post-construction traffic not meeting projections, it's been cut nearly in half from pre-construction levels.[11] In addition, drivers willing to avoid the toll are now detouring through a longer, slower route to use a nearby, untolled bridge. Traffic is up 75% on the free-of-charge-but-slower bridge, despite the pre-construction claims that saved time is the same as saved money.[12]

Beyond tolls and usage charges, we could extend our infrastructure funding approach to include value capture. This is the approach public and private developers for centuries have used to pay for their projects, from Augustus in Rome and Napoleon in Paris to the trading companies given land charters in the New World.

It's largely how Japan has funded its acclaimed high-speed rail system. Buy the land around the station at pre-development prices. Build the high-speed rail, which makes the land far more valuable. Sell the land at the new price and use the profits from the sale to pay for the rail line. This is great public policy, although the lobbyist for the land speculator is not going to be very happy when their anticipated windfall profits end up going instead to the project's investor and risk-taker: the taxpayer.

We can use this same kind of approach for most other infrastructure investments. For example, if we're going to build a new highway interchange or a frontage road, the local government could acquire all the developable land impacted by the project at pre-project prices. Once the project is completed and the land value improved, the local government could then sell the land to the highest bidder and use that revenue to pay for the project.

If that seems a little too authoritarian, understand that this is how most of the United States was originally built. Only, it wasn't government; it was trading monopolies and railroad companies. For the latter, the railroad would acquire land for a town where they intended to put a train stop. As they developed the rail line, they would sell the land around the stop to speculators and use that revenue to pay their capital expenses of building the railroad line. The Long Recession of the 1870s was largely a market correction when railroads overbuilt their systems and the profits speculators counted on didn't materialize.

If this still seems un-American, there's another approach that cities use all the time: the general assessment. If the local government does an infrastructure project that improves the value of a property by $10,000, they may levy an assessment on that property for up to $10,000. There's dual logic to this: It protects property owners from arbitrary taxation by requiring a real improvement in value for the landowner, and it protects the public by having a mechanism preventing public dollars from enriching individuals.

The assessment process could be used by cities or states to capture the private gains that public infrastructure investments make, those dollars being recycled to pay for the project. This is often done for very local projects, although the full cost is generally not assessed. The assessment process is almost never used for major projects, like highway interchanges or light rail stops.

If it were widely used, it would almost certainly kill most projects; our current development pattern does create enough wealth to justify the capital expenditures we make. In other words, private landowners would reject most major projects if they were asked to pay for them. They would reject them because they would lose money.

If we're going to believe in the power of infrastructure spending, if we're going to have faith in the improved efficiency of the market that results from taxpayer investments like these, we should use the feedback from those markets to help us identify worthy infrastructure investments. We don't do this, and within the Infrastructure Cult, such a suggestion is heretical.

That is because, if we did rely on user feedback and real return-on-investment calculations to pick our infrastructure investments, our projects would look nothing like the ones we are currently undertaking, nor the ones we are planning to do.

The Data Doesn't Lie

In 2016, the Congressional Budget Office (CBO) published an analysis that called into question the optimistic rates of return often assumed for federal infrastructure spending, particularly when the money is borrowed, and interest is accrued.[13] This was a rather nuanced white paper, but it undermined a foundational belief of the infrastructure spending narrative: that investments in infrastructure pay a return.

The conclusions of the CBO were hotly contested by some of the nation's leading economists, people for whom a belief in the powers of infrastructure spending has near religious significance. Former Treasury Secretary Larry Summers said the CBO "blew it"[14] and Nobel prize economist Paul Krugman agreed, offering a very specific set of numbers to make the case.[15] When Krugman's scenario is analyzed, only a third of the investment is recovered within three decades, a period when maintenance costs start to overwhelm the wealth produced from those investments.[16] In other words, in the real world, the numbers just don't work.

Summers seems to acknowledge this when, in voicing his disagreement with the CBO conclusions, he predictably indicates (emphasis added):

> I think anyone taking this kind of ground up approach will conclude that the *social return* to public investment is far higher than 2 percent.[17]

Social return. For the Infrastructure Cult, it's where the action is.

The social return can be enormous, and we can develop all kinds of optimistic ways to suggest that it is, but if the investments we're making don't pay a real return – if we don't create enough wealth to pay for the investment and its long-term maintenance – it's not going to matter much. The accumulated weight of negative-returning investments will weigh us down, forcing us to divert more and more of our resources from things that could improve our lives to sustaining systems that never will.

This was evident in an article published by the magazine *Jacobin*, although that's not the conclusion proposed by the author, Doug Henwood. Henwood argued, while citing the ASCE, that the United States is failing to properly invest in infrastructure. He suggests:

> In simple English, the public sector is barely investing enough to keep up with normal decay, let alone doing anything to improve things.[18]

Henwood then provides a chart showing the opposite: nearly eight decades of positive net public investment. The chart shows, decade after decade, total public investments in infrastructure that exceed the amount lost to depreciation. In simple English, even though we now must pay to maintain more than 80 years of public infrastructure – much of it with a negative real return – we continue to build even more.

The CBO only looked at the impact to the federal budget. It didn't consider the impact on state and local governments, which is far worse. While the federal government experiences a general increase in revenue from an overall increase in economic growth, that's not necessarily true for local governments, which rely more on fees, property values, and sales taxes.

And while getting a lower share of the revenue from new growth, local governments assume nearly all the responsibility for the long-term maintenance of new infrastructure. Those costs accelerate over time, while the tax base – built to a finished state – stagnates by design.

It's one thing for the federal government to play this game, but it's quite another for local municipalities. Whether they should be believed or not, there are at least economic theories for national governments to run perpetual deficits, print money, and shun savings. There are no credible approaches, or even potential mechanisms, for cities to operate in this way.

We started with an approach to city-building based on thousands of years of trial and error experimentation, a method that – while not necessarily efficient in its day-to-day operation – was stable, adaptable, and resilient. We now have a new, experimental approach, one where we make transformative investments based on our cultural desires, wrapping them in a veneer of intellectual theory and propaganda math.

The Infrastructure Cult is a byproduct of our approach, not its cause. To fully understand where we are, it's important to understand the fundamentals of why we made the transition from a bottom-up development pattern based on strong neighborhoods to a development approach predicated on top-down infrastructure spending.

Notes

1. https://krugman.blogs.nytimes.com/2016/02/27/the-cases-for-public-investment/.
2. http://larrysummers.com/2017/01/17/the-case-for-a-proper-program-of-infrastructure-spending/.
3. https://obamawhitehouse.archives.gov/the-press-office/2010/10/11/remarks-president-rebuilding-americas-infrastructure.
4. https://www.cnn.com/2015/11/29/politics/hillary-clinton-infrastructure-spending/index.html.
5. https://www.cnbc.com/2017/02/27/trump-pledges-to-spend-big-on-infrastructure.html.
6. https://news.gallup.com/poll/226961/news-public-backs-infrastructure-spending.aspx.
7. Mineta Transportation Institute, http://transweb.sjsu.edu/research/what-do-americans-think-about-federal-tax-options-support-public-transit-highways-and-0.
8. https://www.asce.org/uploadedFiles/Issues_and_Advocacy/Our_Initiatives/Infrastructure/Content_Pieces/failure-to-act-transportation-report.pdf.

9. Ibid.
10. https://www.bloomberg.com/news/articles/2011-08-04/initial-claims-for-u-s-unemployment-benefits-fell-last-week-to-400-000.
11. https://www.in.gov/indot/files/LSIORB%20Project%20Post-Construction%20Traffic%20Study_Final.pdf.
12. https://archpaper.com/2018/11/ohio-bridges-project-louisville-kentucky/.
13. https://www.cbo.gov/sites/default/files/114th-congress-2015-2016/reports/51628-Federal_Investment-OneCol.pdf.
14. http://larrysummers.com/2016/07/14/even-the-best-umps-occasionally-blow-a-call/.
15. https://www.nytimes.com/2016/08/08/opinion/time-to-borrow.html.
16. https://www.strongtowns.org/journal/2016/8/23/makes-us-richer.
17. http://larrysummers.com/2016/07/14/even-the-best-umps-occasionally-blow-a-call/
18. https://www.jacobinmag.com/2017/09/infrastructure-crumbing-public-sector-spending.

5

Growth or Stability

Peasants in medieval England participated in a common-field farming approach that consisted of three great fields. In any given year, the great fields would be designated for wheat or barley, or were left fallow in a rotation understood to maintain optimal soil conditions. By foregoing immediate production and giving a field time to recover, overall yields would be more stable and secure. It was a tradeoff between short-term production capacity and long-term stability, with the peasants opting for stability.

What is more interesting is how these great fields were subdivided among the peasants. Instead of each having their own contiguous section, each peasant would have up to a dozen scattered plots throughout. They would tend to each of these, shunning a consolidation of holdings for an approach that involved burning precious calories walking between plots.

A similar approach has been witnessed in modern times in the Andean mountains of Peru. There the subsistence farmers would likewise scatter their plots over a large area, walking long distances in between to tend to each one. Development experts studying this situation concluded that the Peruvians were paying "intolerably high" costs for all this inefficiency, something more advanced people would not do.

> The peasant's cumulative agricultural efficiency is so appalling . . . that our amazement is how these people even survive at all.[1]

The expert recommendation was to create a land swapping program so these seemingly uneducated, backward peasants could consolidate their holdings and, through improved efficiencies, realize more of the fruits of their own labor.

This was reported in a journal article by researcher Carol Goland, who, with a level of humility not seen in the development experts, sought to understand why peasants would scatter their plots in this way. What she discovered by asking – and then confirmed through measurement and calculation – was that spreading plots is a risk management strategy. In any given year, one plot may be randomly wiped out. Having enough plots, and having them spread out, ensured the peasant family wouldn't starve.

Geographer and historian Jared Diamond examined Goland's research in his book *The World Until Yesterday*. He notes that consolidation of holdings would improve efficiency. Peasant farmers could grow more food using fewer resources and less energy, but they would be – to quote the adage – putting "all their eggs in one basket."

> If your time-averaged yield is marvelously high as a result of the combination of nine great years and one year of crop failure, you will still starve to death in that one year of crop failure before you can look back and congratulate yourself on your great time-averaged yield. Instead, the peasant's aim is to make sure to provide a yield above starvation level in every single year, even though the time-averaged yield may not be highest.[2]

What the efficiency-obsessed development experts didn't appreciate was how fragile their consolidation strategy would make life for the peasant farmers. Instead of being ignorant, the peasants understood a spooky wisdom, insights gained over many lifetimes of trial and error experimentation. The farmers who didn't scatter their plots died. Those who didn't have enough plots also died. The farmers who survived had lots of scattered plots, a strategy for survival they passed on as traditional wisdom.

The development experts were trying to meet a single objective – increasing efficiency – while the peasants were forced to harmonize many competing objectives in an infinite game, one where survival was the ultimate constraint.

Where Does Strength Come From?

The Infrastructure Cult can recommend Americans spend $2.2 trillion at the federal level in order to avoid $1 trillion in local losses because they are focusing on a tiny set of objectives, and not attempting to harmonize many competing priorities. There are understandable reasons for why this myopia developed. I'm going to touch on some of them, but I want to preface that by giving a clear statement on my beliefs.

As an unprovable article of faith, I believe that a financially strong national economy is the byproduct of having financially strong cities, towns, and neighborhoods. I do not believe the opposite: that our cities will be financially strong and healthy if we can only create a strong national economy.

In short, I believe that economic strength is built from the bottom and works its way up, like a foundation supporting a structure. I do not believe that a focus on success at the national level will result in enduring, fine-grained prosperity in our local communities.

I start here with my beliefs in acknowledgment that any conversation about economics today is ultimately a conversation about what one believes. Economics has become our secular national religion, with economists being the shamans of our time. They peer into the statistical entrails whenever we need a one-decimal-point estimate of next year's GDP. They consult disparate signs when we must know whether we should prepare for inflation or deflation.

As within any diverse culture, there are economic priests for all beliefs and attitudes. If you search, you're going to find ones you like and dislike, with no honest way to discern between them other than weighing them against your own values.

My goal here isn't to change your economic religion. What I want to convey are the serious tradeoffs that come with a centralized, nationalized economic strategy. We can have national growth and that has some obvious, positive benefits, but in experiencing growth in that way, we sacrifice some of our local stability. We can increase our local stability, but only if we are willing to sacrifice some national growth.

If we're to work together at the local level to make our places stronger and more prosperous, we're going to find ourselves, at times, purposefully swimming against the currents of national economic policy.

Depression Economics

I'll start with World War I, arguably the greatest turning point for humanity in the post-Enlightenment. The world was one way and then, four and a half years later, it was another. Empires dissolved, monarchs deposed, treasuries drained, and a new experiment in Bolshevism undertaken. It's hard to understate the depth of impact that mechanized killing at such a grand and futile scale had on cultures everywhere.

In the early years of the war, American banks made huge loans to England and France, who used that money to buy war materials, mostly from American companies. The transfer of wealth from

Europe to America would set the stage for the next hundred years. When the United States declared war on Germany in April of 1917, it had a small army barely capable of handling border skirmishes. By the end, millions had been drafted into service. From an economic standpoint, this was all extremely stimulative.

The end of the war kicked off what has become known as the Roaring Twenties, a period of unprecedented prosperity preceding the Great Depression. This was a decade of progressive social policies, technological advances, and easy money. Banks loaned massive fortunes into existence for stock market speculation, a mania that some powerful people tried to curtail but which in the end took on a life of its own, covering up some serious structural problems in the underlying economy.

The fault lines began to be painfully exposed after the huge stock market decline in October 1929, setting off the Great Depression. The interesting thing about the Great Depression is that nobody at the time understood why it happened. We still don't, although many economic denominations claim to have revelatory insight. There were proximate causes to be certain, but it ultimately was the breakdown of a complex system and, thus, any analysis defies a simple cause and effect explanation.

Worse than not being able to point to a cause, there was no clear path to getting out of it. While President Herbert Hoover believed – as many did then and still do now – that the economy would self-correct in time, what he didn't appreciate is that the self-correction of a complex system can be a long and brutal process. And there is no reason to assume it will correct back to anything recognizable. Or desirable. For a representative republic, this belief – right or wrong – seems impossible to adhere to in difficult times.

The New Deal policies of Franklin Roosevelt embraced an attitude of active, large-scale intervention in the economy. Since the exact cause of the hardship was unknown, and the cure even more elusive, the idea was to keep trying things until the economy got better. This generally meant attacking the acute symptoms, particularly unemployment, with national work programs and other centrally directed initiatives.

My late grandfather was a boy during the Great Depression. He spent part of it living with a neighbor family, exchanging his labor for sharing the family's meals and sleeping in the barn. He would go on to join the Marines and be one of the first Americans into Nagasaki after the second atomic bomb was dropped. No weakling, he once told me that he "would be dead" without Franklin Roosevelt and the New Deal. That seemed wrong to me, but I was in no position to argue with him.

With his response to the Depression, Roosevelt was following the economic theories of John Maynard Keynes. One of the truly great minds of the twentieth century, Keynes identified a paradox that has become orthodoxy: Although cutting back on spending during a difficult time was logical for an individual, when everyone did likewise, things quickly went from bad to worse. Called the "paradox of thrift," the corrective response was for the government to step in and stimulate the economy, filling the void left by declining personal spending.

Thus began decades of debate over Keynesian economic policies, a disagreement as unresolvable as it is fundamental. One economic denomination believes that recessions are healthy. Like periodic forest fires or floods are necessary for a healthy ecosystem, the cleansing of a downturn strengthens the economy in the long run. The other faith, the one more aligned with Keynes' views, believes that collective action can minimize – or even eliminate – economic hardship, and that not doing so causes needless loss and unnecessary suffering.

For example, prior to the Great Depression, housing finance was a largely local endeavor. To control risk, local banks dealt in only short-term notes – mostly three to five years – with balloon payments that needed to be refinanced when the loan matured. With capital contracting during the Great Depression, banks were less willing – sometimes not even able – to rollover loans. Many people were unable to obtain new financing when their mortgage expired and the balloon payment came due. This needlessly put them into default, and subjected them to large losses, even when they were making their payments and could afford to continue doing so.

The Federal Housing Administration (FHA) was established during the Great Depression to deal with this problem. The FHA offered mortgage insurance to entice local banks to offer longer-term loans with significantly less money required for a down payment. This allowed people to avoid default, to stay in their homes and continue to make payments. It saved banks from having to sell seized homes into a declining housing market. The FHA stabilized housing prices, which was good for nearly everyone.

The Great Depression's housing crash is a classic deflationary spiral, where collapsing prices – in this case, homes – push otherwise solvent, productive people and businesses unnecessarily into default. This is the kind of unforeseeable event that prompts peasant farmers to spread their plots, and to forgo growth and efficiency for stability. In a modern economy, if there is an obvious case for a Keynesian intervention, this is it.

The Last Country Standing

World War II ended the Great Depression. The mobilization of millions of young men to Europe and the Pacific decreased the supply of workers. Dramatic levels of wartime manufacturing increased the demand for workers. Lowering supply while increasing demand results in increased price. In this case, the price of labor increased, a trend that would continue for the next three and a half decades.

Unlike World War I, where it was unclear until the final months who would win, it became evident sometime in early 1943 that the Allies would defeat Germany and Japan. The only real open question was the cost in lives and treasure. As Allied nations began to contemplate what a post-war international monetary system would look like, the economic trends sending wealth from Europe and Asia to North America accelerated. The United States would be the only major world power to emerge stronger from the war than they went into it.

Prior to World War II, international trade used a system that relied on gold for the settling of international accounts. Countries with trade deficits would deplete their reserves, literally giving up their gold in exchange for getting their own currency back. They now had the same amount of currency in circulation, but less gold, which is a devaluation.

To deal with this, the government would be forced to take money out of circulation, or risk losing all its gold and, by relation, the value of its currency. This is a painful constraint, one that slows the economy. A less enthusiastic economy has less demand for consumption, particularly of imports. With a weakened currency, exporters find their products more competitive internationally. This rebalancing would continue until the country was back in surplus, a point where another country would be in deficit and experience the same painful constraint.

It's that last part – the painful constraint – that made the gold standard very inconvenient for prosperity-seeking, democratically elected governments. If one country is in surplus, another must be in deficit. The friction that reality creates forces them to not get too far out of equilibrium. It can also force them into war.

And when the entire world is at war, or is rebuilding from war, there is no surplus anywhere. The system breaks down.

The Bretton Woods agreement, negotiated in July 1944, established a new international system of fixed exchange based on a gold-backed dollar. Keynes had argued against the gold-backing – some contend to free economies from the constraints of gold-backing, others as a cynical ploy to maintain the power of the British Empire's sterling trading block – but the American negotiators, who literally had the gold, insisted on it. One ounce of gold was set at $35.

The U.S. dollar was now as good as gold and would become the world's reserve currency. To grasp the profound nature of this arrangement, understand that the sale of oil by the Soviet Union to communist China was done in U.S. dollars. Everyone wanting to trade needed dollars, an exorbitant privilege for the last country standing.

The Post-War Boom

Paul Samuelson, Nobel prize–winning economist and perhaps second only to Keynes in terms of influence on modern economics, wrote an essay in 1943 on employment after the war. He stated the consensus opinion among economists at the time, that there was nothing structurally different about the economy that would prevent the United States from sliding right back into depression once the war ended.

> Were the war to end suddenly within the next 6 months, were we again planning to wind up our war effort in the greatest haste, to demobilize our armed forces, to liquidate price controls, to shift from astronomical deficits to even the large deficits of the thirties – then there would be ushered in the greatest period of unemployment and industrial dislocation which any economy has ever faced.[3]

His brilliance notwithstanding, he was, of course, wrong. Not only did the country avoid a return to economic depression, the United States embarked on a multi-decade economic mania that is still looked at as a golden age. America took its industrial capacity and directed it toward building a new version of prosperity, a continent-wide experiment in a new living arrangement.

With the world's reserve currency, abundant and cheap oil, and low individual debt levels, the United States serendipitously found itself with the ingredients it needed for rapid economic growth. What happened was a generation of American growth, two and a half decades of spreading prosperity that is still broadly nostalgized.

In this period of time, Americans built the interstate highway system, the largest public works project in the history of mankind. These transportation investments broke the stifling stability of high land values, making abundant raw land available to the masses at affordable prices. Investments in infrastructure systems accelerated. Through Urban Renewal initiatives, new planning theories were put into practice, remaking entire neighborhoods.

Policymakers quickly discovered that the tools for fighting deflation in the Great Depression worked even better for expanding the economy during the post-war boom. Focusing again on housing, the FHA used the same approach of lowering down payments and insuring banks against default. This time it wasn't fighting a deflationary spiral; it was expanding demand for housing, dramatically increasing prices.

Growing demand for new housing was a boon for the economy. Building this new version of America created millions of jobs, from carpenters and contractors to appliance manufacturers and door-to-door encyclopedia salesmen. A robust housing market created wealth in a growing middle class, a trend that became central to American self-identity. After things had been so hard for so long, everything suddenly became easy.

Of course, it wasn't easy for everyone. The collapse of land values in urban areas resulted in systematic disinvestment – both economically and culturally – in those places left behind. The FHA, along with the government-sponsored housing finance agencies Fannie Mae and Freddie Mac, juiced housing even more by expanding the secondary market, an exchange where local banks could unload qualifying mortgages, freeing lenders up to make more loans.

Large suburban tract homes qualified for the secondary market, but the frugal house with the small attached shop didn't. Anyone who wanted a resilient housing style, one dating back to the streets of ancient Pompeii and beyond, would essentially need to pay cash, a financial handicap that made such investments largely unfeasible.

Any neighborhoods deemed "at risk" also didn't qualify for government support, the left hand of government policy destroying urban land values while the right hand kept people trapped there – at this point, largely economically stressed minority populations – from sharing in the spoils of new growth.

By the time the United States reached the end of the first generation of the post-war boom, the first iteration of what I've termed the *Municipal Ponzi Scheme*, the bulk of the country felt so prosperous it embarked on a massive campaign to end poverty – the Great Society – as it simultaneously fought an expensive war in Vietnam.

By many economic measurements, this is the high-water mark of the twentieth century, particularly for America's middle class. Generations of wealth incrementally built within America's cities had been destroyed in favor of rapid growth and economic expansion, an exchange with a naturally redistributive effect. Individual Americans had experienced how national growth solved their individual problems, a narrative they would never seriously question thereafter.

Struggling with Constraints

The liabilities from this experiment would now start to come due, particularly for local governments. The infrastructure investments being induced created a lot of transactions – a lot of economic growth – but the lack of productivity meant there wasn't enough wealth to maintain everything once the financial sugar high wore off. Cities like Ferguson, Missouri, which was an affluent suburb of St. Louis in the first generation of the post-war boom, now had to sustain all those miles of roads, sidewalks, and pipes with a stagnating tax base not up to the challenge. Ferguson would go on to become notorious for decline and blight, a distinction it shares with most of America's immediate post-war suburbs.

These suburbs became known as "first ring" because, while they began to stagnate and struggle, a second ring of development was being created in the hinterland beyond them. In a manner similar to slash-and-burn agricultural practices, these newer cities gave the affluent a place to move when the signs of stagnation in their first-ring neighborhoods became overt.

This locked in a pattern of growth, stagnation, and decline that would become one of the defining features of the current American development pattern.

At the national level, the French were taking the United States at its word, demanding gold in exchange for dollars as promised under the Bretton Woods agreement. This was a smart move for the French as it was clear the United States was abusing its privilege as a reserve currency, creating more money than was supported by the store of bullion. In theory, declining gold reserves would prompt the government to raise interest rates, reduce the money supply, and slow growth in order to strengthen the currency. Those were painful constraints few Americans welcomed.

Instead, in August 1971, President Richard Nixon "temporarily" ended the convertibility of gold, promising to restore it once the run on gold reserves subsided. The constraining mechanism of gold-backing removed, it has never been restored. Most mainstream economists today consider the need to back the currency with gold, or any other tangible commodity for that matter, an antiquated notion.

A period of prolonged stagflation set in, something that baffled economists. All conventional economic theories suggested that prices rise and unemployment falls during economic expansions, while during recessions the opposite happens; unemployment will rise and prices will fall. Stagflation is a simultaneous rise in prices and unemployment, as if both sides of a see-saw are moving in the same direction in contradiction of the laws of physics.

The nontheoretical response to hardship at the local level was to seek ways to increase efficiency. For example, in my home state we experienced something that has become known as the "Minnesota Miracle." The state government standardized local tax structures to provide one streamlined approach for businesses and individuals. Instead of each city having their own approach, the state would collect property and sales taxes and send money back to cities for essential services, all based on a single formula.

The benefits from this were immediate. Businesses looking to expand no longer had to contend with each local set of parochial regulations. Instead, large corporations were able to tap into a broad set of resources – even Wall Street capital – to make investments and drive growth in a more efficient paradigm. What cities lost in local control they gained in resources as the state, flush with money from new growth, was more generous than stingy, local taxpayers.

There were long-term consequences, however, to the increase in efficiency. Now all cities had the same local tax structure, so a mining community is forced to structure their local economy the same way as an agricultural community, which was the same for a new suburb and for a major, regional center. All local nuance and flexibility were removed, making cities unable to adapt, except in the bluntest ways, as their fortunes diverged.

And once the short-term efficiency gains were realized, the state budget came under its own set of constraints. In the ongoing debates over raising taxes and cutting services, aid to local governments has consistently been the lowest of priorities. Now that local governments' finances are desperately fragile, so is the state government they thought was their benefactor.

Another example of short-term gains through efficiency came with women entering the workforce in increasing numbers. While there were, and still are, strong gender-equity arguments for making the workplace more welcoming to women, it wasn't only liberation that most women were seeking by taking on additional labor outside the home. It was a paycheck, and the increased standard of living that extra income provided.

And, in another example of long-term consequences, that added income didn't ultimately result in broader prosperity and financial stability for families. Over time, it merely increased prices for family essentials, like housing, daycare, and education. Instead of the economy having to adjust downward to meet productivity levels – a painful constraint – women entering the American workforce bailed out the economy by adding their capacity. For economists, another macro constraint avoided.

In the 1960s, a family could live comfortably in the middle class with just one wage earner. Now they need two, at least. We must applaud the empowerment aspect of expanding opportunity for women, and having women in the workplace has benefits beyond economic growth, but it's quite a stretch to think of the person forced to clean hotel rooms, work a gas station counter, or stock shelves at a big-box store, just to make ends meet, as enjoying any meaningful form of liberation.

These actions are akin to the short-term gains from peasants consolidating their plots into a single location. If output is measured in the immediate years following the change, there is little doubt as to the progress being made. When put in the context of an infinite game, however, the increase in fragility becomes the ultimate, painful constraint.

Going All In on Debt

When you're very fragile and you run into hard times, there are only difficult lessons to be learned. That is, unless you can make a deal with your future self.

Debt is future consumption brought forward. We borrow from our future selves with the promise that, when the time comes, there will be some sacrifice to repay the debt. In contrast, savings is consumption deferred. Money that is saved today is a sacrifice that provides opportunity to increase consumption in the future.

As America progressed through the second life cycle of the Suburban Experiment, it took a cultural shift for its citizens to embrace debt. It seems little coincidence to me that this change in attitude coincided with passing of those who were adults during the debt-fueled speculation of the 1920s. Debt increases fragility by making future growth mandatory. If all you've experienced in your life is growth, debt doesn't seem nearly as risky.

Beginning in the mid-1970s, but then accelerating dramatically thereafter, the U.S. economy shifted from one based on growth through savings and investment to growth based on debt accumulation. Government debt is an important part of this story, but perhaps more important is private-sector debt.

In 1980, U.S. households had a 63% debt-to-income ratio. For every dollar in income, a typical family had 63 cents in debt. By 2000, that had grown to 84%, and by 2008, at the start of a financial crisis, family debt was 124% of annual income.[4]

While debt has increased, savings have gone down. In January of 1980, the U.S. personal savings rate was 9.9%. By January of 2000, it was down to 5.4%, and by 2008, it had fallen to 3.7%.[5] Over the past three decades, Americans have borrowed more and saved less.

In classic economics, it is very clear what should happen when there is a lack of savings but a high demand for borrowing: interest rates should go up. That is how the supply and demand of money reaches an equilibrium. When there is not enough savings to meet the demand for borrowing, higher interest rates entice more people to save and fewer people to borrow. Yet, the opposite happened; rates have gone down dramatically.

At the beginning of 1980, when Americans were saving more and borrowing less, the effective Federal Funds Rate of interest was at 13.8%. It would peak the next year at just over 19% and be on a steady decline through three decades of declining savings and increased borrowing. At the beginning of 2000, the rate was 5.5% and eight years later, it was at 3.9%.[6]

There are many theories to explain this, most having to do with the positive impacts of globalization and happy advances in technology. I'm skeptical of the convenience of these theories because they seem to affirm what we want to believe – that our economy is healthy and going to continue growing. I think it more likely that our economy, like the cities that sit at its foundation, is sick and trying to reset to a stable equilibrium.

It is only by robbing our families of wealth – using artificially low interest rates to punish those who save and reward those who borrow – that we've pulled as much future consumption forward as possible. And where our families have fallen short, public borrowing has filled the gap.

I have witnessed countless local governments make up for cash-flow shortfalls with debt. As a professional engineer, without fully understanding what I was suggesting, I recommended many such tradeoffs. If we couldn't pay to maintain a road out of cash flow from our wealth, then borrow the money and turn that cash flow into payments. It solved the immediate problem, I got paid, and – of course – there was the assumption that the prosperity we anticipated in the future would take away any pain our future selves would experience meeting that obligation. Nobody ever analyzed why there were cash-flow problems in the first place.

This is the same logic that underlies the public pension crisis, and it's why it's so intractable. During difficult budget cycles, government employees voluntarily agreed to give up salary and benefit increases. In exchange, they received promises of increased future pension benefits. This was perceived as a great exchange because, of course, the economy was going to continue to grow, the future would be more prosperous than the present, and there would be far more resources to pay those pensions when they came due. Who is now responsible for the failure of that gamble is a question as unsolvable as it is morally ambiguous.

To keep growth going, we sacrificed in the present and we borrowed from our future. Both of those actions only made us more dependent on the realization of that future growth. This is one reason why our economy has become a series of recurring crises and panics whenever growth starts to slow. And it's why we've been more and more willing to cede power to those who could restore us to our unsustainable economic path.

We've been through a savings and loan crisis and bailout, hedge fund failures that threatened the entire market, the runup in Internet stocks with the subsequent crash, and a housing bubble followed by a crisis in subprime lending followed by a re-inflating of the housing bubble. The economic tremors of overreach seem to be increasing in intensity.

Through all of this, the Federal Reserve lowered interest rates all the way to zero and kept them there for nearly a decade, while printing trillions of dollars in digital money in an unprecedented experiment known as Quantitative Easing. This occurred while the federal government ran deficits at levels rivaling those of the world wars. We have brought forward more than a generation of consumption capacity and, in a classic sense, should anticipate a generation of corrective sacrifice.

Right on cue, a new experiment is starting to gain popularity, one that promises to rid us of the few remaining financial constraints. Called Modern Monetary Theory, it promises to deliver growth by embracing the abstract nature of a currency backed by nothing tangible. Under this concept, the centralized government can issue a nearly unlimited amount of currency to pay for whatever lawmakers prioritize. The only constraint is the capacity of workers to mobilize resources in response and our willingness to tax wealth when things go off the rails.

Regardless of the economic religion one subscribes to – be it Keynesianism, supply-side monetarism, debt capitalism, freshwater economics, saltwater economics, New Keynesianism, or

Modern Monetary Theory – the common denominator is the need for more growth as measured at the national level. Ultimately, this is what is broken.

Does Growth Serve Us?

The United States, and by extension most of the world, suffers from a tragic reversal. We once created growth in our economy because it served us. Growth addressed the age-old problem of how to split one loaf of bread between two hungry people: create a second loaf. It is easy to understand how the need to experience economic growth became a national consensus, particularly for the generation that lived through the Great Depression and World War II.

The tragic reversal comes from the realization that growth once served us, but now we serve growth. The constraint of modern America is that we must experience annual growth in our economy. Without growth, we can't service our debts, pay our retirements and pensions, and keep up with the rising costs of health care and education.

For a long time, the Suburban Experiment presented an easy solution to this problem. By pouring money into highways and infrastructure, by making it easy for families to buy new homes in distant places and by establishing funding mechanisms for the mass development of commercial real estate, we experienced the longest and most robust economic boom in human history in the decades after World War II.

Yet, each iteration of new growth creates enormous future liabilities for local communities, a promise that the quickly denuding tax base is unable to meet. Not only did these new areas need police and fire protection, street lights, libraries, and parks, but all those miles of roads, streets, sidewalks, curbs, and pipe; all those pipes, pumps, valves, meters, culverts, and bridges would eventually need to be fixed and replaced. At the local level, we traded our long-term stability for near-term growth.

As one example, the city of Lafayette, Louisiana, had 5 feet of pipe per person in 1949. By 2015, that had grown to 50 feet, an increase of 1,000%. They had 2.4 fire hydrants per 1,000 people in 1949, but by 2015, they had 51.3. This is a 2,140% increase. Over that same period, median household income in Lafayette grew just 160% from an inflation-adjusted $27,700 to $45,000.[7] And if national trends hold locally in Lafayette, which they almost certainly do, household savings decreased while personal debt sky-rocketed. Lafayette grew its liabilities thousands of times over in service of a theory of national growth, yet its families are poorer.

Today, nearly every U.S. city has a backlog of routine infra-structure maintenance they will never be able to perform. This represents miles of street that won't be fixed, and huge lengths of pipe that will never be replaced. This infrastructure serves the homes and businesses of Americans. It is the foundation of their personal wealth. Ultimately, none of that will matter.

In pursuit of growth nationally, we have rendered our cities financially insolvent. The base assumption of all our theories seem to be that a strong national economy would trickle down to strong cities, towns, and neighborhoods. This belief held true whether the trickle-down mechanism was large government or large corporations, government spending or tax cuts, the empow-erment of centralized bureaucracies or centralized corporations. America's leaders seemingly believed that, if we strengthened the top, it would strengthen the bottom.

This is an incorrect understanding of how complex, adap-tive systems grow stronger. In such systems, strength and stabil-ity are always built from the fractal level. Successful blocks beget successful neighborhoods. Prosperous neighborhoods make up a prosperous city. A strong and stable state is an assembly of strong and stable cities.

In *Cities and the Wealth of Nations*, a book I believe presents the most insightful economic analysis since Keynes, journalist and author Jane Jacobs describes how cities, not nations, are the only coherent level of economic analysis.

Distinctions between city economies and the potpourris we call national economies are important not only for getting a grip on realities; they are of the essence where practical attempts to reshape economic life are concerned.[8]

A measurement of GDP tells us as much about American prosperity as a measurement of the average wealth of a hundred households when one of those households includes billionaire Jeff Bezos. How does a measurement like inflation have any credibility – or real meaning – when health care, college tuition, home prices, and construction costs have increased annually for decades at rates much greater?

What is lost in all the centralization and efficiency is local nuance, or what most people would consider real meaning.

The Difference Between Growth and Wealth

Going into the summer of 2005, there was general concern among economists and money managers that a recession was imminent. The yield curve was flattening as investors bought longer-term notes to lock in higher rates ahead of possible interest rate declines.[9] The Dow Jones average was down 7% from the start of the year.[10] The Federal Reserve was raising rates to get some wiggle room should the anticipated rate-cutting stimulus be needed.[11]

Indicators were moving in the wrong direction, and then at the end of August came Hurricane Katrina, which destroyed large portions of New Orleans and the Mississippi Gulf Coast. A few weeks later, Hurricane Rita hit much of this destruction a second time. It was terrible, and like many Americans, I felt a sense of embarrassment over America's seeming inability to do much to make things better.

I would later have a chance to see some of the neighborhoods in New Orleans that were most impacted by Katrina. Entire blocks were wiped out, generations of accumulated wealth destroyed. Yet, what happened to GDP in subsequent months is telling. Here are the statistics as presented by the Congressional Budget Office:

Estimated Net Effect of Hurricanes Katrina and Rita on Real GDP (billions of 2005 dollars at annual rates)

2005, Second Half: –21B to –33B
2006, First Half: +24B to +36B
2006, Second Half: +35B to +48B
2007, First Half +33B to +47B
2007, Second Half +27B to +35B[12]

The overall economy takes a hit immediately after each hurricane, but in the two years that follow, these disasters are a major stimulus. All the cleanup and rebuilding, all the recovery spending and one-time consumption, is a boon for the economy.

That is the dichotomy. What is good for a national economy is not well aligned with what is good for a local economy. The national economy is focused on growth, a short-term metric that is not correlated with real wealth or broad prosperity. In contrast, a local economy depends on wealth accumulation, a long-term reality that correlates to stability.

If we worried about the national economy and didn't care about what it meant for cities, local businesses, or families, we'd just pick a few random cities to destroy each year and reap the economic benefits of rebuilding. If we worried about our local economies, we'd obsess about real wealth creation, not growth.

It is relatively easy to optimize one or two economic variables at the national level, at least in the short-term, if we're willing to ignore fragility or tolerate absolute failure in other realms. What our cities desperately need today is a more nuanced approach to capital investments, growth, and development, a harmonizing of objectives that can only happen effectively at the local level.

Ultimately, building a prosperous America is a hyper-local undertaking. Yet, hyper-local undertakings are messy and chaotic. They can be dominated by small-minded thinking, by parochial concerns. In a society as connected and outwardly affluent as ours, where experts in all realms peddle their own low-pain rescue remedies for the challenges we face, American society has developed a low tolerance for the messy and chaotic.

A Paradox of Thrift or Avarice?

Keynes identified the *Paradox of Thrift*, the damage done to the national economy when individuals and organizations save instead of spend during an economic downtown, but what about the opposite? What about a *Paradox of Avarice*, where individuals and organizations don't save but spend all they have? And more. What are the impacts of such a condition?

To serve us, to attempt to solve the great problems humanity has long struggled with, we created an economy that produces growth. When growth is an option, it is a fantastic thing. When we experience growth, it often makes our lives easier. It solves problems and can add to the comfort and beauty around us. Growth is good.

Yet, we have gone to the next step and made continued growth a condition of our prosperity. It is no longer merely a positive experience but a prerequisite for our comfort. And if we should experience a period where we fail to grow, or even grow at rates lower than what we had anticipated, then all manner of hardship is visited upon us.

Czech economist Tomas Sedlacek posed the question: Do we want an economy to be more like a person standing or a person riding a bike?[13] A person standing is stable. They can move forward but moving is not required for stability. In contrast, a person on a bike must keep moving forward if they are to stay upright. For the person biking, standing still is unstable.

They must continually move ahead, something that is ultimately impossible in an infinite game.

The economics of a traditional city was like a person standing. It could grow, even very rapidly, but it was also stable without growth. Growth was a positive condition, but not a requirement. In contrast, the post-Depression American city is increasingly like a person on a bicycle; it must keep growing, at ever accelerating rates, or things fall apart.

In the past, growth served us. Today, we serve growth.

In the system we have evolved, the ideal citizen creates growth, not by saving and investing, but by consuming beyond their means. It matters little that this is ruinous to the individual, that such financial insecurity creates enormous levels of instability. Individual avarice is necessary for our national GDP to grow. Savings is punished with artificially low returns while debt is subsidized. Our individual value to the whole is based on our capacity, even our desire, to consume.

Local governments are induced to take on unpayable long-term liabilities so that the national economy can experience growth today. In the name of efficiency, they are stripped of nearly all means of ingenuity. Our cities orient up the government food chain, allowing themselves to be positioned at the bottom, grateful for the crumbs they receive. This is backward.

To build Strong Towns, local leaders will need to take steps to opt out of these systems. This is difficult because it's the water we all swim in, and the current gets stronger as things become more desperate. Still, if we are to truly serve the people in our communities, and by extension be there when we discover we need all seven of our scattered plots, we need a new path to prosperity.

Our cities must now intentionally sacrifice growth in order to have stability. In the infinite game we are playing, stability is a requirement, growth an option.

Cities are a collection of us; they are the way we take collective action in our communities. Over the past century, we've gradually given up this responsibility, deferring the direction of our places to the priorities of others. If the people are to lead again, if we're to create a prosperous future for ourselves and our neighbors, local government must reassert leadership.

Notes

1. https://www.jstor.org/stable/3673760?read-now=1&seq=19#page_scan_tab_contents.
2. Jared Diamond, *The World Until Yesterday* (New York: Penguin Books, 2012).
3. https://fraser.stlouisfed.org/files/docs/publications/books/posteconprob_harris_1943.pdf.
4. St. Louis Fed, https://fredblog.stlouisfed.org/2015/01/on-household-debt/.
5. St. Louis Fed, https://fred.stlouisfed.org/series/PSAVERT.
6. St. Louis Fed, https://fred.stlouisfed.org/series/FEDFUNDS.
7. https://www.strongtowns.org/journal/2015/9/14/lafayette-pipes-and-hydrants.
8. Jane Jacobs, *Cities and the Wealth of Nations: Principles of Economic Life* (New York: Random House, 1985).
9. https://money.cnn.com/2005/07/12/markets/bondcenter/bond_yields/.
10. http://futures.tradingcharts.com/historical/DJ/2005/0/continuous.html.
11. https://money.cnn.com/2005/08/09/news/economy/fed_rates/index.htm?cnn=yes.
12. "The Macroeconomic and Budgetary Effects of Hurricanes Katrina and Rita: An Update" (Washington, DC: Congressional Budget Office, September 29, 2005).
13. Tomas Sedlacek, *The Economics of Good and Evil: The Quest for Economic Meaning from Gilgamesh to Wall Street* (New York: Oxford University Press, 2011).

6

Rational Responses

Our cities made decades of bad investments, sacrificing their stable wealth in exchange for new growth as part of a continent-wide experiment. Most local governments are functionally insolvent, having more long-term obligations than they have revenue potential. They react to this imbalance by trying to grow even more.

The fundamental lack of financial productivity in our development pattern has made our governing systems fragile, despite our best intentions. Calls for more efficiency, greater centralization, and much more spending reveals a lack of awareness, along with an embedded desperation. This can't continue.

I've presented these facts hundreds of times, to audiences big and small, across the North American continent. The most common question I receive is also the most predictable: What is the solution?

People have gotten angry with me, quite indignant, over this. Once, at the end of one of my lectures, someone stood up and yelled at me, "Chuck, you've come here and scared us all. Don't tell me you did this without a solution in mind. What are we supposed to do? What's the five-step plan?"

Of course, I have ideas of what we should do, but I don't have any magic that can keep decades of bad investments from unwinding. Much of what happens next is already baked into the North American cake. I've heard Chris Martenson, economic researcher and author of *The Crash Course*, frame an answer to a similar question in this way on his podcast:

> Problems have solutions. Predicaments have outcomes. This situation has moved beyond a problem into a full-blown predicament. We need to stop trying to come up with solutions and instead shift to a conversation about managing outcomes.[1]

If a solution requires that we maintain every road that has been built, that we rehab every leaky pipe, that we hold on to all the neighborhoods that have been developed – and in most places today, these are prerequisites for any conversation – then there is no viable solution. Our cities are going to contract geographically; we will have fewer lane miles, fewer pipes, and less urbanized land in three decades than we do today. This is built into the math, shifting the situation we face from problem to predicament.

That answer rarely goes over well, and I'm going to acknowledge up front that, for many people, such a viewpoint feels defeatist. The United States didn't become a great nation by retreating in the face of adversity. A great people have the ingenuity to overcome any challenge. All we need to do is unleash the American spirit of creativity, entrepreneurship, and determination and we'll figure it out.

That's one narrative, but it's not my narrative. The United States of America became a nation by following a leader, George Washington, who was widely known for strategic retreats. Yes, there is great ingenuity among Americans, but history demonstrates that necessity is the mother of invention; overlooking the hardship that spurns innovation is simply a way to comfort ourselves with confirmation bias. Overshoot, followed by a consolidation of gains, is a common experience throughout human history.

We're not going to keep and maintain every cul-de-sac, interchange, or frontage road that has been built. It's not possible and, even if it were, propping up these places is a poor use of our resources. In a very real sense, many of our infrastructure systems are going to completely fail, whole neighborhoods will be abandoned, and cities will shrink geographically. Some of what has been built in the past two generations will be salvaged for reuse, but I suspect that much of it will simply rot in place.

This seems incomprehensible to us today, particularly to those living in the newest homes and shopping in the latest strip mall in the distant suburbs or exurbs. Yet, there is a continent-wide precedent in recent memory that we've culturally explained away as a one-time anomaly, that being the abandonment of cities by the affluent after World War II.

If we could have talked to a family living in an urban neighborhood in the 1930s and told them that, within a decade, they would pick up and move out to a field on the far outskirts of town, they would have been appalled. Except in a few places where the trend had already started, the outskirts was where the poor people lived.

Even more to the point, that family had deep connections to the neighborhood they were living in. It was likely that they had immediate family as neighbors. They had church, school, civic organizations, work, and all their social connections within walking distance. Leaving all that would have seemed unthinkable at the time, yet that is exactly what most of them did.

Affluent Americans walked away from cities when it became apparent that there was a better deal to be had somewhere else. When our policies began tipping the scales toward the growth that came with rapid suburbanization, urban neighborhoods went into decline. Those who could move, did. It should be no surprise to anyone that, as many of these post-war neighborhoods inevitably end up in decline, those who can move to more prosperous areas will also do so.

If there were no social costs, we could think of this process as a long overdue trimming of an overgrown shrub, something awkward in transition but ultimately healthier and stronger. There are huge social costs, however, and they can't be ignored. More to the point, they won't be ignored.

A Long Decline

I've encountered a predisposition to assume that the imbalances I've described must lead to a crash, some type of rapid phase shift from one state of existence to another. A fragile bridge will still carry traffic up until the moment it collapses, the random point where there is one innocuous vehicle too many. It felt like our economy was trying to collapse in 2008, a result that would have painfully exposed how fragile we are. I don't rule out the possibility of such an event in the future. They do happen.

What I think is more likely, however, is a long decline. Unlike a collapsing bridge, a road fails slowly over time, the small problems accumulating until they aggregate into a broader failure. In some ways, long declines are more pernicious than collapses because we culturally excuse away each step, finding ways to adapt to continually worsening outcomes. There is no singular, mobilizing event shared by all but more of a malaise that creeps across society, a general dysfunction that can be blamed on a variety of convenient scapegoats. Indeed, blaming is part of the decline, a critical feature that fuels it along the path.

Social commentator and author James Kunstler best described this process as a "long emergency," an ongoing breakdown of the complicated mechanisms that enable modern life. He points out how difficult it can be for a broad culture to identify the underlying predicament and instead become stuck focusing on the solutions that have plausibly explainable problems. In his words:

> This is perhaps a self-evident point, but throughout history, even the most important and self-evident trends are often completely ignored because the changes they foreshadow are simply unthinkable. That problem is sometimes referred to as an "outside context problem," something so far beyond the experience of those dwelling in a certain time and place that they cannot make sense of available information. The collective mental static preventing comprehension is also sometimes referred to as "cognitive dissonance," a term borrowed from developmental psychology. It helps explain why the American public has been sleepwalking into the future. The Long Emergency is going to be a tremendous trauma for the human race.[2]

Modern Americans have a track record of explaining away the process of decline. The term *white flight* is an unnecessarily narrow description applied to the depopulation of core cities and the explosion of horizontal growth following World War II. While there is no question that race was an accelerator in the process, and practices like redlining went beyond class to systematically disenfranchise minorities, affluence was the underlying factor driving the mass migration. In a broad sense, people with means and agency decamped from cities, leaving behind those who lacked that option.

I make this distinction because, as despotic as that outcome was for those left behind, it pales in comparison to the conditions being created on the current trajectory. When poor people were left behind in the center of Americans cities, they still lived in coherent neighborhoods. The places they inhabited still mostly resembled successful human habitats. Despite the decline and disinvestment, people living in these neighborhoods could walk to find food, live in a neighborhood with family and friends, and make a living in the economic ecosystem that immediately surrounded them.

As the affluent abandon declining suburbs today, the poor left behind face a whole new dimension of struggle. Now, amid decline and disinvestment, they must deal with a development pattern designed with an assumption of permanent affluence.

To get around, one must have a car. While it is possible to walk from the cul-de-sac, through the ditch, across the berm, around the drainage pond, over the four-lane road at an unmarked crossing, and then across the parking lot, all just to get life's essentials, it's not like that can be done without a huge commitment in time, not to mention unpleasantness.

Try hauling your purchases through that same trip in reverse. Now do it during difficult weather. Now do it while raising young children, caring for an elderly family member, or dealing with an illness. For the disadvantaged, this kind of environment magnifies all of life's struggles.

A bike can make things a little easier in terms of time, but with a huge tradeoff in safety; infrastructure designed for high-speed automobile travel is treacherous for people on bikes.

In post-war America, the cost of an automobile is the ante for living a productive life. It is extremely difficult to hold a job, find food, educate children, seek medical assistance, be part of a church or civic organization, or do any of the routine things that humans do without a motor vehicle. Burden poor families with the cost of an automobile and it starves them of essential resources, accelerating decline.

Individual homes require intensive, ongoing maintenance. For families already financially stretched, in neighborhoods prevented from changing or evolving to a higher state of intensity, where is that time and money going to come from? The resources aren't there, and so homes begin to fail, dragging down entire neighborhoods.

There is also a sad irony to much of the maintenance of modern development. Traditional building materials require a base level of ongoing maintenance, tasks perfectly suited for the low-skilled worker willing to learn a trade. Modern maintenance-free materials don't have these ongoing costs, which seems like a good thing, until they fail. That's when they impose a huge replacement cost.

As Steve Mouzon points out in *The Original Green*, mainte-nance-free simply means not able to be maintained. There is no patching or hacking maintenance-free systems; they either work or they fail.

> When so-called "no maintenance" materials fail, they fail catastrophically so you have to replace every bit of the materials, not just the damaged piece.[3]

As mentioned in Chapter 2, auto-oriented places have different failure mechanisms than traditional neighborhoods. In the latter, rising underlying land values create natural reinvestment opportunities. That mechanism doesn't exist – there are no rising land values – in the slash-and-burn style of building, and thus there is no natural incentive for reinvestment. Once a home fails, it drags everything around it down, creating a negative feedback loop that won't be arrested without massive outside intervention.

Someone living in a declining neighborhood is going to receive all the signals that the decline will continue. In such a place, only a fool would invest their time or limited resources in fixing up their home. If it costs $5,000 to fix the leaking roof in a declining neighborhood, that is money that will never show up in improved resale value, so why do it? Why paint the faded siding? Why replace the broken sidewalk? Even if the means to address these problems existed, every logical financial incentive is to merely struggle with the symptoms of decline.

And this is all before considering the local government, who is now tasked with maintaining all the roads, streets, walks, curbs, pipes, pumps, valves, and meters – infrastructure they couldn't afford to maintain when things were shiny and new – with a tax base in decline and an impoverished population struggling to get by.

To make matters worse, aging cities routinely take on debt to compensate for their insolvency. Unlike federal and, to a lesser extent, state governments, debt levels are a genuine constraint for local governments. Too much debt crowds out other spending and only serves to magnify the despair of decline.

There was a lot written about why Ferguson, Missouri, blew up in riots and a police crackdown following the shooting death of Michael Brown during a police incident. Most of this analysis involved race. Again, I'm not dismissing race as an accelerating factor, but Ferguson – one of the early post-war suburbs – is a case study in building a place designed to decline.

Ferguson was one of the suburbs of St. Louis built in the first generation of automobile expansion. It was once shiny and new, attracting the affluent and middle-class who were partaking in the American dream. It enjoyed a generation as one of the premier places to be in the St. Louis region, until the end of the growth phase and the predictable decline began to manifest.

The affluent in Ferguson long ago departed for newer places with better prospects. The middle-class exodus happened during Ferguson's second life cycle – the stagnation phase – as public debt rose and decline spread. Those with public pensions stuck around a little longer, which partially explains how a city populated by mostly minorities ends up with a police department that is nearly all white.

Forget strategic investments in growth; Ferguson today is so indebted that it can't maintain its basic infrastructure systems. In the year Brown was killed, the city spent over $800,000 making interest payments on their debts while allocating only $25,000 to the maintenance of sidewalks.[4] There are good reasons for Ferguson residents to walk in the streets; their sidewalks are falling apart.

Beyond the built-in nature of decline in a specific place, there is a regional aspect to decline that is equally pernicious. Many regional infrastructure systems require maintenance of the oldest components for the newest to function. For example, with a sewer system, the new pipe in front of the exurban home requires the old pipe downstream in the core neighborhood to function. Water systems, drainage, and much of our transportation networks function in this same way.

The opposite does not hold, however: The older parts of the system do not need the newer. The infrastructure within the core, urban neighborhoods of a city can function regardless of what happens to the infrastructure out on the edge. In many cases, if the edge neighborhoods went away, the core infrastructure would function better.

In other words, there is a floor on how low the level of disinvestment in infrastructure can be in traditional neighborhoods without the entire system collapsing, but there is no systematic threat to disinvestment out on the edge. The roads and pipes throughout America's suburbs can completely fall apart and, with few exceptions, it will have no impact on the infrastructure within the urban center.

Whether we want it to happen or not, the accumulated liabilities of cities are forcing them into a long decline. In the triage of what is maintained and what can rot away, there is a cold, logical rationale for contracting cities around the traditional urban core and its immediately surrounding neighborhoods. This is reinforced when the affluent leave declining areas on the edge and start to reinhabit core neighborhoods.

Restoration of Normal

The North American development pattern mass-adopted after World War II is a massive experiment. Americans transformed an entire continent in mere decades, discarding centuries of wisdom on how human habitat is constructed in favor of new ways of doing things. Trillions of dollars were mined out of, or reallocated from, traditional cities to feed a growth machine that built a middle class, and then trapped them in financial purgatory.

The traditional orientation of cities, the pattern that persisted in the United States and Canada since European settlement up until the twentieth century, can still be seen in most cities outside of North America. In these places, wealthier people generally live near the center of the city while the poorer people live toward the outer edge. This is reflected in underlying land values, which place a premium on the more centralized and accessible places.

After World War II, trillions of dollars were spent in North America inverting this historic pattern, moving the affluent to the edge while leaving the poor trapped behind. As the financial systems that induced the change become frayed, as the weight of accumulated liabilities overwhelm our attempts to keep things propped up, it seems likely – even natural – that cities, and the regions around them, would start to revert to something like their original form.

In that sense, trends toward re-urbanization of the affluent become even more understandable. In his 2012 book *The Great Inversion and the Future of the American City*, Alan Ehrenhalt describes shifting living patterns that were already being experienced around major North American cities.

> The most powerful demographic events of the past decade were the movement of African Americans out of central cities and the settlement of immigrant groups in suburbs, often ones many miles distant from downtown.[5]

Ehrenhalt identifies a trend that has only accelerated in the intervening years:

> We are moving toward a society in which millions of people with substantial earning power or ample savings will have the option of living wherever they want, and many – we can only guess how many – will decide in favor of cities and against distant suburbs. As they do this, others will find themselves forced to live in places less desirable – places farther from the center of the metropolis. Statistics from the U.S. Census Bureau in October 2011 revealed that in the first decade of the new century, poverty increased by 53% in the nation's suburbs, compared to only 26% in the cities.

Not only are there increasingly more impoverished people living in the suburbs, but the number of neighborhoods with extreme levels of poverty – census tracts with poverty rates of 40% or more – doubled between 2000 and 2010, with America's suburbs experiencing the greatest amount of that growth.[6]

Simultaneous with the rise of suburban poverty is the gentrification of urban neighborhoods. As well-located urban land values rise once more, the value of the improvements on those properties also goes up. This is a mechanism that historically created new wealth, but it no longer works that way.

Zoning codes established for the rapid replication of the auto-oriented development pattern were also applied to urban neighborhoods. These codes do not allow neighborhood evolution; their central feature is to "protect" existing property owners by locking the current development pattern in place. For example, a neighborhood of single-family homes must remain a neighborhood of single-family homes. The person living there is unable to turn higher property values into a redevelopment opportunity that expands the number of units.

With demand driving land values up and the neighborhood pattern scaled in regulatory amber, the most likely outcome to bring the *Improvement to Land Ratio* back into balance is to demolish the existing home and build something equivalent, only at a high-end price point. This is commonly called a "scrape off" and the net effect is to dislocate the existing population.

All of this can be seen in hyperreality in a city like Detroit, which I've described as being an early adopter of the Suburban Experiment and, thus, a demonstration of one likely path American cities will take.

The urban core of Detroit has seen tremendous revitalization, with mega-project public investments in stadiums and infrastructure complimented by private investments in office towers, hotels, and condominium units. These neighborhoods are becoming increasingly exclusive with poorer residents being priced out to more suburban areas.

There are also pockets of affluence out on the far edges of the community, where newer suburban investments – including malls, big box stores, and single-family residential subdivisions – are still in the first-generation, Illusion of Wealth phase of development. In many ways – metaphorical but also sometimes literal – these areas are walled off from the rest of the region. Depending on their ability to use their political influence to garner continued government subsidies, these may be the last holdouts of a vanishing way of life.

In between the core and these remote strongholds of affluence sits a vast area in transition. Most of this transition zone is overwhelmed with despair, with neighborhoods vanishing as the homes burn, rot, or are razed. There is no real land value and so all the natural financial mechanisms for renewal are absent. The modest wealth that remains is being systematically destroyed. These are not happy places, and it is jarring to the senses to see them.

Within this despair, however, there are pockets of wealth creation where – in places that seem mostly random and unpredictable – people have come together to form small, interconnected neighborhoods. In many ways these new neighborhoods resemble the first iteration of my hometown that I described in prior chapters. There are frequent use of common walled structures, multiple ways to make a living, essential goods and services within walking distance, eyes on the street policing, and many of the other resilient characteristics found in traditional development patterns.

It is these new neighborhoods that I find so inspiring, that I think we can learn a lot from. For a city with such a depth of poverty and wide chasms of wealth inequality, these special places hold the promise of renewal. Like a seedling emerging in the springtime, these places need to be nurtured, but not overwhelmed with affection.

I was present at a speech given in 2016 by Detroit Mayor Mike Duggan where he promised that no Detroit neighborhood would be left behind. While it was an absurd statement that belied every discernible fact on the ground, I'm fine cutting the mayor some slack. Even today, there is no cultural dialogue in Detroit about intentional neighborhood abandonment. There is no room for the mayor to state the obvious.

And so a destructive cultural farce ensues, one that demands the allocation of scarce resources to places with no future, while the areas of despair continue to atrophy, the people in them trapped in a feedback loop of decline. We must do better.

Paramedics are trained in the practice of triage. The process arose during wartime when there were too many patients for the medical systems to handle. As difficult as the triage conversation is – and we're talking here about the lives of heroes shattered on a battlefield – it is obviously necessary and, ultimately, compassionate.

Triage divides patients into three categories. The first is those who are likely to live, regardless of what care they receive. These patients become a low priority because they can fend for themselves, at least until more urgent needs are addressed.

The second category are those patients who are unlikely to live, regardless of what care they receive. In extreme triage cases, these patients are abandoned. In less urgent situations, compassionate steps are taken to ease the suffering of those whose passing is imminent.

The final group is those for whom immediate care might make a positive difference in outcome. For triage personnel, this is where the maximum effort is made. It is these people who we can snatch from death. It is this group of patients to whom we can give a higher quality of life. In financial language, these are high return-on-investment scenarios.

If we can have this conversation about human lives, we can have it about neighborhoods. We can have it about roads and pipes. We can have it about garbage collection and fire protection. And we can do this with intention, giving our actions the maximum opportunity to align with our compassion, in contrast to the low expectations of a long decline.

Our cities must embrace the challenging task of harmonizing competing objectives. This is not easy, but it's what leadership will look like in the coming generation.

Making Difficult Decisions within a Complex, Adaptive System

Once we accept the cities are complex systems, we are forced to come to grips with the reality that we can never fully understand them. More to the point, what we often think of as simple and obvious solutions to the problems we face are simple and obvious *only because of* our limited understanding. The more we truly know, the less clear things become.

Which neighborhoods are likely to survive the long decline? Which neighborhoods are likely to decline? Most importantly, where in the unknown will new neighborhoods coalesce? It's tempting to put a theory in place and charge ahead. After all, this is how Americans have operated for the past three generations (and, arguably, humans prior would have acted if given the same means for transforming their habitat).

Wall Street trader turned author and philosopher Nassim Taleb suggests that there are confident ways to live in a world you don't fully understand. They begin with acknowledging the limits of our capacity to predict the future. From his book *The Black Swan*:

> If you know all possible conditions of a physical system you can, in theory, project its behavior into the future. But this only concerns inanimate objects. It is another matter to project a future when humans are involved, if you consider them living beings and endowed with free will.
>
> If you believe in free will you can't truly believe in social science and economic projection. You cannot predict how people will act.[7]

Prediction is a central feature of modern public policy, particularly for cities. Yet, with complex systems, prediction provides false comfort. Again, from Taleb:

> Artificial, man-made mechanical and engineering contraptions with simple responses are complicated, but not "complex," as they don't have interdependencies. You push a button, say, a light switch, and get an exact response, with no possible ambiguity in the consequences. But with complex systems, interdependencies are severe. You need to think in terms of ecology. . . .
>
> In the complex world, the notion of "cause" itself is suspect; it is either nearly impossible to detect or not really defined.[8]

Our cities now lack the resources to compensate for prediction mistakes. We can't pretend to know the future and we're too fragile to place huge bets on a specific outcome. We are like that primitive farmer knowing we need seven different plots but realizing we have only one. We're going to have to innovate a new approach.

Curtis Carlson, a corporate CEO who now works with organizations on improving innovation, is credited with a statement on innovation that aligns with Taleb's insights. Dubbed "Carlson's Law," it goes:

> In a world where so many people now have access to education and cheap tools of innovation, innovation that happens from the bottom up tends to be chaotic but smart. Innovation that happens from the top down tends to be orderly but dumb.[9]

I think it's rather clear that Americans prefer "smart" over "dumb," yet time and again, Americans – especially the more affluent ones – have an even stronger preference for order over chaos. We have the luxury of tolerating a lot of dumb in the pursuit of order.

If you doubt this, think back to the last time you sat at a traffic signal in the middle of the night. You can see in all directions, there are no cars anywhere in sight, yet you wait for the light to turn green. You sacrifice your own ability to think and act independently on your judgment, as well as your time and fuel, for the sake of order. This is so accepted it's done without any thought given to the tradeoff.

Complex systems maintain order at the macro level only because they have some chaos at the fractal level. Ecosystems do not become stable by suppressing volatility but by experiencing it regularly at levels designed to make the system stronger. This is the core of Taleb's antifragile insight.

Traditional cities weren't stable because they lacked chaos; they were stable because routine difficulty forced the community to constantly adapt, to continually harmonize competing objectives. To say it another way: Things were tough and so people had to work together to figure it out. When they did, they survived and potentially thrived. When they didn't, those places went away.

Nobody at the state and federal level is going to solve the problems we face in our local communities. Yes, there are things that can be done – and I'm going to outline some of them in subsequent chapters – to make rebuilding easier, but the recipe for the strengthening of America's cities is not something that will be bequeathed from on high. We must do that, together, starting in our own neighborhoods.

Therefore, the rational responses we seek to this broad set of challenges must emerge from our efforts. If we're going to respect the complex, adaptive feature of cities, it is that emergent nature that must be the humble takeaway. We must resist the imposition of grand solutions and the instant implementation of a big idea.

The great urban planner Daniel Burnham said, "Make no little plans; they have no magic to stir men's blood," and to that I generally agree. I would add, however: Take only incremental actions; they alone expose the flaws in our thinking that allow us to ultimately reveal true wisdom.

Many people have suggested to me that the challenges we face are so overwhelming that we must take grand action. They insist that the threats we face, including those outlined thus far in this book, are so monumental that working incrementally, allowing responses to emerge over time, is simply not an option.

I believe the exact opposite: The problems we face are so enormous, so intertwined and multifaceted, that the only way to approach them with a full appreciation of the stunning level of complexity they hold is incrementally.

We're starting from a point where no civilization has ever been. No society has ever conducted an experiment of this magnitude on itself, transforming not only the development pattern of an entire continent, but literally discarding the knowledge for how to build the habitat that co-evolved with us. There is no guidebook for us to follow. The path ahead from where we are today is not clear.

If we're going to have broad American prosperity, if we are to experience the comfort and stability of being truly strong and successful, Americans must again embrace a chaotic but smart approach to evolving our cities. To harmonize competing interests in a successful human habitat, our response to these stresses needs to emerge from within, not be imposed from the outside.

Notes

1. https://www.peakprosperity.com/
2. James Howard Kunstler, *The Long Emergency* (New York: Grove/Atlantic, 2005).
3. Steve Mouzon, *The Original Green: Unlocking the Mystery of True Sustainability* (New Urban Guild Foundation, 2010).
4. https://www.strongtowns.org/journal/2014/8/25/stroad-nation.html.
5. Alan Ehrenhalt, *The Great Inversion and the Future of the American City* (New York: Vintage Books, 2012).
6. https://www.brookings.edu/testimonies/the-changing-geography-of-us-poverty/.
7. Nassim Nicholas Taleb, *The Black Swan* (New York: Random House, 2007).
8. Nassim Nicholas Taleb, *Antifragile* (New York: Random House, 2012).
9. https://www.nytimes.com/2011/06/05/opinion/05friedman.html.

7

Productive Places

A few blocks from my home there is a restaurant with several historic photos hanging on the wall. I've seen them many times but had never stopped to look closely at them, until one day I was waiting for a table and my eyes lingered on a photo of a circus parade passing through a historic downtown. It was a fantastic scene.

The stagecoaches were traveling in procession down the middle of the dirt street. Crowds had turned out to watch the spectacle; they were standing on the wooden walkways, lining the public realm. The men were wearing suits and hats while some of the women had parasols. A few kids ventured out into the street, many holding hands with an adult.

As a person, I loved the energy of the space, but as an urban planner, I also marveled at the design. The buildings lined up to create a strong edge. They were perfectly spaced across the street at the just the right ratios to create that sense of place. The structures themselves were grand: two and three stories with strong vertical proportions and pleasant symmetry, all with subtle ornamentation. The stores opened onto the street, with large windows, sometimes covered with awnings and balconies.

I was in awe of this place, and then I realized it was a photo of my hometown from 1904. A handwritten inscription near the top read, "West Front Street, Brainerd Minn." It was a street I knew well. Yet, while Front Street was a mere block from where this photo hung, the image I was looking at was a world away.

I obsessed about the photo to the point of figuring out exactly where it had been taken. I placed myself there and captured an updated image. The contrast is stark. Front Street is now a collection of mostly empty parking lots and modestly occupied buildings. There are few reasons to congregate on today's Front Street, and even fewer people doing so. The grandeur is long gone, replaced by a sense of desolation.

During my lectures, I often display these two images in sequence as an example of how the experimental development pattern has impacted cities. One time, when I was speaking at Boise State University, a student raised their hand after that sequence to provide a comment.

This young man informed attendees that he was from Costa Rica, that his was a very poor country, and that they could not afford to build the way he experienced cities being built in the United States. According to him, Costa Ricans must build their cities one block at a time. Before they can build a second block, they must make sure that every gap on the first block is being used, otherwise they won't be able to afford it. He reiterated that Costa Rica was a very poor country.

The people who built that street in 1904 were poor as well. More accurately: They did not have an abundance of resources to waste on mistakes. The Costa Rican student was describing the approach used by cultures who are aware of their own fragility. For him, the waste and unproductivity of the modern

American development pattern is disorienting. Only the richest country in the world could build so much and make such poor use of it.

The United States is now a very poor country as well, especially our local governments. Yes, there are pockets of extreme wealth, and there is a lot of money velocity to provide the illusion of progress, but we do not have resources to squander. We must act like our ancestors, taking incremental steps in the dark.

This may sound scary, but it's actually liberating. Looking at that photo of the 1904 street, one realizes that these people did not have zoning codes. They did not have approval processes, boards, and committees to oversee construction. They weren't forced to invest in miles of pipe and streets in order to have "shovel-ready" sites. They didn't spend their time chasing state and federal grants. They didn't hand out tax subsidies. They likely didn't employ any engineers, planners, or economic development staff.

They didn't have any of the tools that we have come to believe are essential to building a successful place, but there it was. They didn't even have 30-year mortgages, yet this collection of lumberjacks managed to build a place deep in the northern woods of Minnesota that was not only spectacular to behold, but financially productive, adaptable, and full of economic opportunity.

The way they did this is easy: They copied what they knew worked. They took the materials they had on hand and they built using an approach that had been proven successful over thousands of years of refinement. They made modest investments over a broad area over a long period of time, growing their city incrementally upward and incrementally outward, all while evolving to become incrementally more intense.

Every city, every neighborhood, has this same capacity for incremental improvement. There is nothing preventing any North American community from growing stronger, wealthier, and more prosperous. Nothing.

A Simple Math Problem

The urgent constraint we must address is one of simple math. In the infinite game of building a community, our ongoing expenses currently exceed our ongoing revenues. Our liabilities exceed our wealth. To address this math problem, our wealth must increase and/or our liabilities must decrease to the point where our ongoing revenues exceed our ongoing expenses. That math is as humble as it is merciless.

If we were only dealing with a math problem, however, it would be easy. Human habitat is about far more than math. It includes the messy interpersonal relationships, the complex cultural context, and the historical civic commitments that we have made to each other. In short, we must fix the humble math problem while simultaneously harmonizing multiple competing objectives. That's what it means to build a real place.

This is where the mechanical professional approach gets in the way. Among urban planners, and many other city-building professionals, there is a consensus that increasing density is a solution to most problems. Density can be measured in dwelling units per acre or people per acre; it's the same concept. The theory is that, if we add more units or more people, the financial situation will be improved, which will give us the resources to solve other problems.

I'm not a fan of the density metric. My sense is that density, at best, is a byproduct of success, but never the cause. I've seen horrible developments built with optimum density, but terrible design and site location. I've also seen beautiful, low-density construction that was financially viable and well integrated into the community. Success may correlate with density but building density does not cause success.

Focusing on density is comfortable for today's professionals because it allows them to continue within the current development paradigm. Density is accomplished by building large projects, all at once, to a finished state. It maintains the illusion of cities as static models, where mechanical variables can be calculated, predicted, and planned, without all the messy feedback loops. This is not the way complex, human habitat works.

Instead of density, the math we must focus on is the relationship between private investment and public investment. Is there enough private investment to support the community's public investments? Said another way: When we build or take over a community obligation, do we have enough private wealth to financially sustain that commitment?

When I examine the farm where I grew up, the answer is: yes. The farm was very low density and it didn't generate a lot of tax revenue for the community. It also didn't cost very much. The only public infrastructure was a road, of sorts, something slightly more intense than a two-tire path through the field. For the city, this was absolutely a cash-flow-positive situation, despite the low density.

On the other end of the density spectrum, consider the Empire State Building in New York City, which is appraised at $2.5 billion.[1] There are a few million dollars of asphalt, concrete, and pipe in front of the Empire State Building's entrance, infrastructure that is essential for the functioning of the building. The likelihood that this street will deteriorate from lack of funding is very small. The possibility that the Empire State Building will be abandoned from lack of water or sewer service or inadequate street access is nearly zero. There is plenty of wealth in the building to justify, and accomplish, maintaining the essential infrastructure.

There is no information on what a financially viable ratio of private to public investment looks like. When I used to do engineering work for developers, a common pro forma metric was that infrastructure costs would be roughly 5% of the home cost. That's a 20:1 private to public ratio, assuming the infrastructure would become a municipal obligation.

What this doesn't take into consideration is all the common infrastructure that can't be attributed to a specific property, things like traffic signals, interchanges, arterial roads, lift pumps, and water towers. As a rough rule-of-thumb, modern development patterns require equivalent levels of investment in common infrastructure and site-specific infrastructure. While this varies based on the extent of horizontal development – as in West Coast cities, which are more auto-oriented and thus spread out, will be higher, while more compact East Coast cities will be lower – an equivalent investment means a private to public investment ratio of 40:1.

These are targets, and I think knowledge of optimum ratios will evolve over time as our cities transform. In the near-term, however, a prudent target ratio of private investment to public investment will be somewhere between 20:1 on the risky end and 40:1 on the secure end. If a city has $40 billion of total value when all the private investments are calculated, sustaining public investments of $1 billion (40:1) is a doable proposition. Public investments totaling $2 billion (20:1) starts to be risky with outside forces of inflation, interest rates, and other factors beyond the community's control threatening to impact potential long-term solvency.

This ratio is important because we're done adding infrastructure. Any community serious about their own financial stability is going to take the obvious first step and stop adding more liability. There is no reason for any North American city to build another foot of roadway, or put in another length of pipe, to serve any new property anywhere. Our infrastructure is maxed out; we're done expanding and, in fact, I anticipate nearly all our cities contracting their obligations to some extent.

Our challenge now is not about expanding our infrastructure networks but making better use of what we've already built. We must put meat on the bones, so to speak, a shift in focus to building more wealth within the framework of our current investments.

To make that happen, we first need to understand where our wealth lies.

The Financial Strength of the *Old and Blighted*

In my hometown, there are two identical blocks along a roadway in the core of the city. They are separated by a single block. We can think of one of these blocks as *Old and Blighted* while the other has been transformed into something *Shiny and New*. They sit on the same thoroughfare. They abut the same neighborhood. They are the same dimension, have the same area, and are serviced by the same amount of public infrastructure. They are identical except for the development style.

The *Old and Blighted* block is a collection of pop-up shacks built in the 1920s. At that time, these three blocks sat on the far edge of town. These were the small experiments of their day. As my city was growing incrementally, these three blocks were the next increment outward. The people who built these pop-up buildings certainly anticipated that, as the city grew, their land values would increase and these cheap, one-story buildings would be expanded and improved. That had been the pattern of development for cities for thousands of years.

Of course, that is not what happened. Within a decade of these blocks being built, the country entered the Great Depression, then World War II, and then launched a new economic model with an experimental pattern of urban development. These three blocks were passed over in favor of new development further out on the edge of the city. They have stagnated in a state of development infancy for nearly a century.

The city government labeled these blocks as "blighted" and, in the official planning documents, called for their redevelopment. They identified the specific types of businesses they would like to have instead of the ones currently there. In what they labeled the General Commercial area, they indicated:

> The intent of this designation [General Commercial] is to provide areas for highway-oriented businesses. Examples of these could include highway-oriented businesses such as fast food restaurants, convenience stores, gas stations and other auto-oriented businesses as well as a number of large retailers.[2]

After this designation was made, the city received an application for redevelopment and subsequent construction of a fast food franchise called Taco John's. This development was approved, the old buildings removed, and in their place the new drive-through restaurant was built. The taco franchise not only met all the development goals of the city, it complied with all the zoning and development regulations. In terms of vision leading to plan and then to implementation, this was a home run.

On that, everyone seemed to agree. The city was able to get rid of blight. In its place was now something shiny and new, which was exciting. There is now plenty of convenient off-street parking. The city was able to remove the on-street parking, which allows the traffic to now flow more quickly. There is even a new sidewalk and a bit of greenspace. These are all welcome signs of progress.

While the *Shiny and New* block is now a Taco John's franchise, the *Old and Blighted* block remains a collection of marginal commercial businesses. There are nine businesses on 11 lots within that old block, including a pawn shop, a bankruptcy attorney, a couple liquor stores, an old-time barber shop, and a neighborhood-oriented restaurant. This is some of the most marginal commercial real estate in the entire region.

Here's why all of this is important: The *Old and Blighted* block has a total value of $1.1 million. Add up the taxable value of each of those businesses and that is what you get. In comparison, the *Shiny and New* block, which has the same dimensions, same amount of public infrastructure, and same everything except for the development style, has a value of only $620,000.[3]

In terms of community wealth, the *Old and Blighted* block is 77% greater than the *Shiny and New*. The old block generates 77% more property tax than the new. Despite outward appearances, the *Old and Blighted* is far more financially productive, even though it costs the community the same to service.

The *Old and Blighted* block is the traditional development pattern – the way civilizations around the world built human habitats for thousands of years – in its infant phase, after suffering nearly a century of neglect, and it still outperforms the stuff we are building today. And it's not even close.

Not only is the *Old and Blighted* the financial winner, it outperforms in many other ways. Those 11 small businesses have 11 local owners. That's 11 entrepreneurial people deeply vested in the community. I interviewed them all; collectively, they employ another six full-time equivalent positions. The Taco John's franchise, which is headquartered two states away in Wyoming, would not tell me how many people they employed in their Brainerd location. Their application to the city indicated between 20 and 25, almost all of which are part-time employees.

Six of the small business owners in the *Old and Blighted* block indicated that they hire a local accountant, someone within the city limits. Two use local attorneys. Seven use one of the local printing shops. Six advertise in local publications. These are dollars passed around the community to employ my friends and neighbors. The Wyoming-based Taco John's franchise would not indicate to me where they obtained similar services. I suspect they find it more efficient to source those services outside of Brainerd.

And all of this while the Taco John's is still shiny and new. What happens when it ages, when the sign fades, the siding starts to show its age, and the parking lot has weeds growing up in the cracks? This very development suggests an answer.

The Taco John's has a new building, but it was not a new franchise in Brainerd; it merely moved up the street three blocks to a new location. It left behind a building in disrepair on a site in a state of decline. After years sitting empty, that old site experienced a succession of failed businesses. The current iteration is a restaurant serving Asian cuisine. The site has been cleaned up, but few would call it thriving.

Why would the Taco John's franchise choose to relocate three blocks instead of fixing up their old location? The answer is simple: tax subsidies. With the corridor labeled as blighted and designated for highway-oriented redevelopment, Taco John's could receive subsidies – in this case, a 26-year Tax Increment Financing subsidy – to abandon their old site and redevelop the new. While the Taco John's is paying 44% less taxes in its new location than the businesses on the *Old and Blighted* block, for nearly a generation it will get those taxes returned to them as part of the redevelopment agreement.

Let me summarize: In exchange for 26 years of tax relief, the community was able to get an out-of-town franchise restaurant to abandon their old building and move three blocks up the street where they tore down a block of buildings and replaced them with a development that is 44% less valuable than the development pattern of what was removed. By any financial measure, this is a bad investment, yet cities everywhere routinely do this exact kind of transaction.

Downtown versus the Edge

In my home region, the most valuable properties are along the highway corridor, a state highway that provides a bypass around the core of the city. The frontage roads along the highway provide access to the standard collection of big box stores, strip malls, and franchise restaurants. The most valuable of these is the 22.8-acre Mills Fleet Farm complex, a site that includes a double-sized big box store, an auto dealership, and a gas station.

Mills Fleet Farm was founded as a general store in downtown Brainerd. Their relocation to the highway corridor, and their expansion to big box locations across the Midwest, is a source of local pride. When Mills officials show up at a local council meeting, their concerns are given full attention. Sometimes more. With a site valued at $14.4 million, they are one of the largest single taxpayers in the region.

In contrast to the success along the highway bypass, downtown Brainerd struggles. In the four and a half decades I've been alive, no new buildings have been constructed in the core down-town. Plenty of buildings have come down, some voluntarily and others as a result of fire. These empty spaces are now used as parking lots. While great strides have been made in recent years, the downtown struggles with vacancies at the ground level. Most of the second and third stories are unused or should be, given their condition.

The nine square blocks of the core downtown constitute 17.4 acres. The 132 separate properties within the core have a combined tax value of $18.9 million.

In a farm field, productivity is measured in terms of output per acre. For example, the productivity of a wheat field is mea-sured in bushels per acre. Land is the base resource of our cities, and financial productivity should be examined in this same way. What is the value per acre created by different development pat-terns? How productive are the neighborhoods we build?

Mills Fleet Farm receives the deference that comes with being a huge taxpayer, but their financial productivity – the value their development creates per acre utilized – is relatively low. The $14.4 million dollars of tax value spread out over 22.8 acres yields a financial productivity of just $630,000 per acre. They pay a lot of taxes, but they use a *lot* of land, all of which is served by expensive roads, pipes, and drainage systems.

The core downtown uses less acreage and yields a greater tax base. That's impressive, but the financial productivity is truly astounding. The $18.9 million of the downtown on just 17.4 acres has a productivity of $1.1 million per acre. Even with decades of decline, disinvestment, and tax-base loss, the financial productivity of the downtown is 72% greater than the most suc-cessful site out on the highway bypass.

How much was spent getting the Mills Fleet Farm and the other sites along that corridor? The state of Minnesota, accessing federal dollars, spent hundreds of millions on the highway bypass. Millions more were spent on frontage roads, backage roads, pipes, pumps, water towers, and the like. This infrastructure now becomes the infinite obligation of various governments, regardless of any changes in the financial productivity in the adjacent private land.

How much did present-day generations spend building the wealth that has endured in the core downtown? The reality is: very little. That was wealth my great-great grandparents and their contemporaries built incrementally over time. They bequeathed it to us as an endowment of sorts, a base of such amazing financial productivity that we could continue to rely on it through times of prosperity as well as times of struggle. We've slowly milked it down, yet tremendous wealth remains.

Someday, Mills Fleet Farm will no longer be at their current location. It may be 5 months, 5 years, or 50 years, but at some point in the future, Mills Fleet Farm will relocate or simply close altogether. What becomes of this site when that happens? A look around the community, and others nearby, suggests an answer.

A rash of big box closings have left many similar sites vacant. In these cases, it's not uncommon for the owners to request a reduction in their valuation, which they are entitled to, despite the anxiety it creates. The market value of commercial property is tied to revenue; for a vacant store, there is no revenue. Even where it is argued that the tax value should be based off the level of investment, a big box store – despite the size – is a marginal investment.

Construction costs for big boxes are generally less than $50 per square foot.[4] For comparison, the National Association of Home Builders reports average construction costs of $85 per square foot for new, single-family homes.[5] An office or retail building can be expected to cost between $100 and $150 per square foot.[6] Corporations build big box stores because they are cheap, and that makes them easy to amortize in a short time frame and ultimately easy to abandon.

Where big box stores are reused instead of abandoned, the iteration after the big box tenant will generally be of lower intensity and lesser value. Warehousing, government buildings, and churches are all common. These uses pay fewer taxes, where they pay any at all. It is almost certain that Mills Fleet Farm, in its present state, is the peak of financial productivity for this site. It is likely to never be worth more and has a very good chance of ultimately being worth much less.

In contrast, what happens when one of the 132 properties in the downtown loses a tenant? What happens when a business owner retires? Or grows to need a larger space? Or must downsize to a smaller space?

What happens when the market shifts and there is too much retail space and not enough office space? Or too much office space and not enough residential?

In the core downtown, none of this change is a problem. Despite the ornamentation, the buildings are very simple boxes. If spaces are too big for the current market to utilize, internal walls can split them into smaller units. If more space is needed, internal walls can come down. There is an enormous amount of flexibility.

Buildings can easily shift from one use to another based on what is needed. I've seen some of these storefronts shift from retail, to a restaurant, back to retail, then to office space. There is an amazing amount of flexibility in this pattern, an ability to adapt as the market changes.

In the traditional development pattern found in my downtown, nobody needs to be able to predict the future. We don't have to guess right to be successful; adaptability means there is no huge downside to being wrong. Out on the highway bypass, the lack of flexibility means there is tremendous downside to being wrong; entire sites will be abandoned, despite the public investment in place.

Out on the edge, we have a development pattern that is expensive to build, low in financial productivity, and is fragile, lacking the ability to adapt without massive infusions of additional capital. In the core of the city's traditional neighborhoods, we have a development pattern that is built incrementally over time, with high financial productivity, and is strong, with the ability to adapt and change with market conditions.

There is a reason our ancestors, around the world, for thousands of years, built human habitat in this way. We were both playing an infinite game; the only difference is that they were aware of it.

Value per Acre

When I was consulting with cities as an engineer and a planner, I worked to make sense of the financial implications of individual projects. Engineers are trained to estimate costs, and so I was good at calculating how much expense the cities I worked for would incur in different development styles. I later taught myself how to calculate revenue streams so I could analyze the real return on investment for individual projects. What I was lacking was a way to expand these insights beyond the inferences that could be drawn from single projects and into a holistic examination of development patterns across an entire city.

This all changed when I met Joseph Minicozzi, an architect and urban planner living in Asheville, North Carolina. Joe is the founder of Urban3, a cutting-edge firm doing data visualization, property tax analysis, and return-on-investment modeling. Our work is so complementary that we have not only become frequent collaborators, but also deeply committed friends. There are few people as generous as Joe and I am extremely grateful for the time we have spent together.

Urban3 is best known for their three-dimensional models of financial productivity. Before I ever looked at Taco John's, Mills Fleet Farm, or the core downtown of Brainerd, they were doing similar analysis for entire cities.

While I talk about productivity in terms of farm fields, Joe talks about gas tanks. When considering the fuel efficiency of a vehicle, it is absurd to think of it in terms of miles per tank. Just because a vehicle has a big fuel tank doesn't mean it's using gasoline productively. We all understand that the most productive vehicle is going to be the one that gets the most miles per gallon. The hybrid Prius is going to make more productive use of gasoline by getting you further per gallon used than the Ford F-350.

For cities, land – particularly land served by expensive municipal infrastructure – is the finite resource. How productive a community is in utilizing that resource has a direct bearing on the community's wealth and its capacity to endure in this infinite game.

One of the early models Joe put together was in response to criticism a colleague of his was receiving. His colleague was redeveloping a dilapidated building downtown and, as part of a street renovation project, benefited from a sidewalk widening and some decorative benches placed in front of his building. Critics called this an unwarranted subsidy and pointed to the local Walmart as an example of a business operating in the free market, without subsidy. Joe did the math.

Like Mills Fleet Farm, the Walmart is a large taxpayer, but it consumes 34 acres of land, all of which is provided with permanent municipal utilities. The downtown building under renovation sits on just 0.2 acres of land. It is also served by utilities, albeit at a very different level of intensity.

Table 7.1 shows Joe's apples-to-apples analysis of financial productivity for these sites:[7]

Table 7.1 Comparison of Walmart versus Downtown Redevelopment

	Asheville Walmart	Asheville Downtown Building
Land Consumed (acres)	34.0	0.2
Total Property Tax per Acre	$6,500	$634,000
Total Sales Tax per Acre	$47,500	$83,600
Residents per Acre	0	90
Jobs per Acre	5.9	73.7

In every measurement of productivity, the downtown building vastly outperforms. It pays nearly 100 times more property tax per acre. It pays 76% more retail taxes per acre. It has 12 times the jobs and, on top of it all, people live in the downtown building. Nobody is living at Walmart, at least not legally.

It takes only 2.6 acres developed to the intensity of that single downtown building for Asheville to raise as much revenue as the entire 34 acres of the Walmart site. That's the same return at a fraction of the financial commitment, with a model that is more adaptable and resilient over time.

The team at Urban3 has modeled hundreds of cities around North America. This massive data set has revealed a near-universal set of trends, results that are consistently observed in cities of all sizes, in all geographies, using all taxing systems, across the continent. These include:

- Older neighborhoods financially outperform newer neighborhoods. This is especially true when the older neighborhoods are pre-1930 and newer neighborhoods are post-1950.
- Blight is not an indicator of financial productivity. Some of the most financially productive neighborhoods are also the most blighted.
- While there are exceptions for highly gentrified areas, poorer neighborhoods tend to financially outperform wealthier neighborhoods.
- For cities with a traditional neighborhood core, the closer to the core, the higher the level of financial productivity.
- The more stories a building has, the greater its financial productivity tends to be.
- The more reliant on the automobile a development pattern is, the less financially productive it tends to be.

The traditional development pattern – even when blighted and occupied by the poorest people in our communities – is financially more productive than our post-war neighborhoods, regardless of their condition. Across North America, our poor neighborhoods tend to subsidize our wealthy neighborhoods. Generally, the places this doesn't hold true are communities where the poor have been displaced out to the edge.

None of this would surprise our ancestors. One evening, Joe and I were wandering through the library at Harvard's Graduate School of Design, where Joe had done his graduate work. We were browsing town planning books from the late 1800s and early twentieth century. Repeatedly in these publications, we came across a simple metric they used for measuring success: value per acre.

I have a civil engineering degree, a graduate degree in urban and regional planning, and decades of experience. Joe has an architecture degree, graduate work in planning, and a similar level of experience. We were never taught about value per acre. It is lost wisdom, abandoned along with so many of our ancestors' hard-gained insights.

Lafayette's Return on Investment

The outstanding question that many technical professionals have for me about the value-per-acre analysis is how closely it correlates to the actual return on investment. Value per acre looks at wealth creation, but a full return-on-investment analysis would examine both the expenses and revenues associated with different development patterns. Skeptics dismiss value per acre for this reason.

There is a powerful rationale to prefer the value-per-acre heuristic: It's simple math. A full return-on-investment analysis, on the other hand, is a massive undertaking. It involves looking at all of the many sources of revenue a city has, the multiple types of ongoing expenses it incurs, and then allocating those to properties to make a comparison. For every hour spent doing a value-per-acre analysis, we would need to spend dozens to analyze a similar area with a return-on-investment calculation.

I've been involved in enough projects, and walked enough neighborhoods, to have a lot of confidence in the value-per-acre approach. Even so, there is a lot at stake for professional experts, public officials, and large developers; each have strong incentives to prefer their intuition over mine when it comes to large investments and big projects out on the edge of town. Therefore, when asked to assist Urban3 in doing a full return-on-investment analysis for the city of Lafayette, Louisiana, I jumped at the opportunity to put value per acre to the test.

It passed the test, of course. It took us a year to produce a profit and loss map for the city, a graphic analysis that combined the revenue associated with each parcel with its expense. The map had the same basic pattern as the value-per-acre analysis. Parcels with high financial productivity – high value per acre – tended to be profitable, or closer to profitable, than other properties. The historic center of the city, and some of the surrounding core neighborhoods, were cash-flow positive, while the edge was dramatically cash-flow negative. The further from the center, the worse the financial shortfall became.

Beyond validating value per acre as a heuristic, the Lafayette project was stunning for the insights it provided. Perhaps the most jarring were the top line numbers; Lafayette has $16 billion in total tax base but $32 billion in public infrastructure. Instead of a private investment to public investment ratio between 20:1 and 40:1, Lafayette's is 1:2. Two dollars of public investment have only produced one dollar in taxable wealth, a stunning lack of financial productivity. I'll note that, in terms of North American cities, there is nothing abnormal about Lafayette's development pattern.

The median family in Lafayette pays $1,500 per year in taxes to the local consolidated government. For the local government to make good on every promise they have made – to fix every street, maintain every pipe, take care of every drainage system – taxes for the median family will need to increase to

$9,200 per year. That is one out of every five dollars a family makes, just to keep what they have.

That will never happen, and so like cities further along this experiment – places like Detroit – the people of Lafayette are going to make decisions on what they maintain and what they let go, what neighborhoods they hang on to and the ones they allow to fall apart.

To say these are difficult cultural conversations is understating the obvious, but there is a wrinkle common to many cities like Lafayette that makes this dialogue even more problematic. When we did the research, we found that the newest neighborhoods out on the edge were the most financially insolvent. However, everything there is relatively new – they are in the Illusion of Wealth phase of their development cycle – and so, until something must be maintained, these edge neighborhoods are cash-flow positive.

In contrast, the core neighborhoods – those neighborhoods that are very poor and blighted but also very profitable over the long term – have suffered from decades of decline and neglect. The infrastructure there is falling apart; the neighborhoods are desperately in need of investment. They have generated plenty of cash to pay for their basic maintenance, but it has been squandered in other places, largely subsidizing new growth out on the edge.

For the dispassionate observer, it's pretty clear what needs to happen: The free cash flow from the edge development needs to go to shoring up basic infrastructure in the core neighborhoods. When the edge developments require maintenance, those should be the places where the public obligations are wound down.

Lafayette is a municipal corporation. If it were run like a corporation, this would merely be a necessary shifting of resources from a failing division to a profitable one, a way to strengthen the overall corporation. We don't generally run our incorporated municipalities like corporations, however. It's hard to imagine the affluent – in their newer homes on large lots paying substantial taxes out on the edge of town – voting for local government officials that promise to intentionally abandon their cul-de-sac to free up the cash needed to make substantial improvements to the high-crime, poor neighborhoods.

The merciless nature of the math suggests this will be resolved in time. How that happens is as unclear as it is inevitable.

Personal Preferences

While I find it silly and tiresome, I feel compelled to address the most common critique I receive on the value-per-acre analysis: It doesn't take personal preferences into account. As often stated to me, many people prefer to live in a single-family home on a large lot along a cul-de-sac. They don't want to live within traditional neighborhoods in close proximity to other people. Americans want big box stores, strip malls, and fast food, not corner stores and mom-and-pop restaurants. Or so it's stated.

Ironically, this critique comes most often from professional staff working for local governments, as if their role isn't steward of the municipal corporation but something more akin to customer service, with a customer-is-always-right ethos.

Let me state the obvious: Every personal preference comes at a price point. I prefer lobster to hamburger, trips to Europe over camping at the state park, box seats over sitting in the outfield upper deck. I choose to enjoy hamburger, camping, and the view from the cheap seats because I value my money more than my first preference. I don't lament this choice – I truly love a good burger, camping with the family, and a day at the ballpark – but I know that, if I had unlimited funds, my preferences would be expressed differently.

Let me make another obvious observation: Since the end of World War II, public policy at every level of U.S. government has focused on subsidizing the purchase of single-family homes. If the government were willing to subsidize lobster to be cheaper than hamburger, I'd continuously dine on lobster. More to the point, I'd express a strong personal preference for lobster. The longer this subsidy went on, the more entitled my expectations for lobster would become.

Middle-class housing subsidies and transportation spending are the bread and circuses of modern America. Americans express a preference for single-family homes on large lots along cul-de-sacs because that's the lifestyle we subsidize. We've been willing to bankrupt our cities, and draw down the wealth prior generations built, in order to provide that subsidy. It can't go on indefinitely.

As a voter, as a property owner within a municipal corporation, as a person living cooperatively with my neighbors in a community, I can respect that some people prefer development styles that are financially ruinous to my city. My local government should not feel any obligation to provide those options, particularly at the price points people expect.

Living in a Strong Town is a cooperative effort, one where everyone is welcome. Even so, the process of harmonizing competing objectives in an infinite game means that some development options now widely available to Americans will no longer be available at price points people have come to expect. Those able to process that basic truth are going to be best positioned to adapt to what comes next.

Notes

1. http://www.empirestatebuildinginvestors.com/25-billion-empire-state-building-appraisal-6.html
2. City of Brainerd Comprehensive Plan, https://www.ci.brainerd.mn.us/DocumentCenter/View/797/Brainerd-Comprehensive-Plan-2004-PDF.

3. This is all original data I gathered from the county's public website as well as my own interviews with business owners. It is documented at https://www.strongtowns.org/journal/2012/1/2/the-cost-of-auto-orientation.html.

4. https://www.chainstoreage.com/wp-content/uploads/2013/07/ConstructionSurvey_2013.pdf.

5. http://www.nahbclassic.org/generic.aspx?genericContentID=260013/.

6. https://proest.com/office-building-construction-costs-per-square-foot/.

7. Data provided by Urban3, https://www.planetizen.com/node/53922.

8

Making Strong Investments

Our cities need to be done with building horizontal infrastructure. We already have more public obligations than can be supported by the private wealth in our communities. There is no informed reason why we would add more promises we can't keep. The challenge we now face is making productive use of that which we've already built. In the infinite game of building human habitat, that is a complex undertaking. In the realm of public investment, it requires an entirely different model.

Cities must run at a profit. They must create 20 to 40 dollars of private wealth for each dollar of public infrastructure liability. In North America, thousands of once-prosperous neighborhoods are now locked in a cycle of decline. In others, large flows of capital have overwhelmed existing development patterns, artificially inflating real estate prices and dislocating many. Our challenge now is to use the resources we have to more productive ends.

Doing this in complex human habitat, where the goal is not merely to become financially strong and resilient, but to do so while harmonizing an infinite number of competing objectives, presents a paradigm-busting challenge. The systems we've built to replicate the post-war development pattern are so effective, and so embedded in society, that is it difficult to conceive of an approach that places stability above growth.

Starting with our most financially productive neighborhoods, we must become far more sophisticated and purposeful in the way we make public investments.

The Barbell Investment Approach

Any American who opens a private investment account is subjected to a series of questions designed to help them ascertain their comfort with risk. It's not clear to me if the Securities and Exchange Commission has mandated this or if the legal counsel at brokerage houses collectively determined this was a good defensive measure. Either way, the correct answer to the long stream of questions is the same: medium.

Do you want to invest in a company specializing in crypto-genetic-tech or do you prefer a money market account? Are you more comfortable putting your nest egg on red at the roulette wheel or would you prefer to bury it in the backyard? The questions are designed to let investors know that there are high-return approaches that come with a lot of risk as well as low-return approaches that are safer.

And most of us prefer medium. Most investors desire to take some risk in order to have some upside potential in their portfolio, but they don't want to be reckless. Medium seems prudent, like wearing khaki pants and a blue sport coat yet donning a splashy tie. Or a black dress with pearls. It's grounded, yet with a little bit of embellishment. It feels right.

Unfortunately, the medium investor is the sucker at the card table, the one unlikely to experience more than modest gains but to suffer disproportionately when things go poorly. They have little upside potential but lots of downside risk. They invest heavily in index funds to capture the long-term compounding of the market without understanding the decades-long gaps between market highs, corrections, and a return to the prior high. There is comfort in the crowd. Medium.

Sophisticated investors protect themselves from loss while simultaneously exposing themselves to upside potential. They are never going to have the anxiety of suffering great decline, but they do have a reasonable chance of experiencing significant gain. They do this by avoiding a medium approach and instead clustering their investments into two extreme categories: very low risk and very high risk.

This is sometimes called a "barbell strategy" because of the embrace of the two ends of the risk profile (Figure 8.1). A barbell investor deploys most of their wealth in boring, low-risk ways. Their objective is to have little chance of losing money, with a near certain chance of making a small amount. The rest of their investing is of the riskiest variety, stuff that has the potential to completely flame out but could also shoot the moon. The latter allocation is where the portfolio's upside potential comes from.

If a barbell investor puts 90% of their portfolio in the safest assets, they have limited their exposure to loss. If everything in the risky end of the portfolio fails disastrously, the most they can lose is 10%. However, if some of those risky investments do well, the upside potential is tremendous. Turn 1 dollar into 10 on the risky end and the portfolio nearly doubles. Turn 1 into 100 and it is transformative.

The traditional development pattern captured the dual risk profile of the barbell strategy. Mature neighborhoods were safe stores of wealth, a repository the community could rely on. They were strong and resilient, unlikely to fail catastrophically. The newer neighborhoods incrementally growing on the edge were the high-risk, high-reward investments; little was lost if they failed but the community gained disproportionately when they were successful.

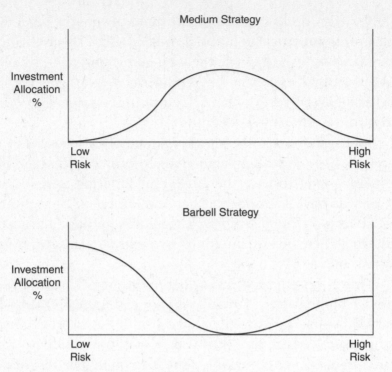

Figure 8.1 Investment Allocation for a Medium Strategy and for a Barbell Strategy

In the infinite game of city-building, where we need to harmonize competing objectives within complex human habitat, following the barbell investment strategy is a way to allocate common resources with minimal risk yet still have a lot of upside potential. It fits with a strategy of incremental change where triage from overexpansion is being forced upon us.

Low-Risk Investments with Steady Returns

The low-risk side of our public investment portfolio is as obvious as it is boring: Local governments must prioritize basic, routine maintenance in neighborhoods with high financial productivity (high value per acre).

For example, the downtown of Lafayette should never want for basic sidewalk maintenance. Those poor neighborhoods next to the downtown should never have streets full of potholes, overgrown ditches, or backed up pipes.

In Lafayette, these high-productivity neighborhoods are cash-flow positive. In cities more atrophied than Lafayette, the highest value-per-acre neighborhoods may not be profitable, but they have the best chance of becoming so, better than any other neighborhood in town. This is where our greatest wealth is; all we need to do is stabilize it.

Most cities prioritize maintenance based on the incorrect assumption that they are going to maintain everything they have built, that it is all worth maintaining, and that any future short-falls they anticipate can be solved by future decision-makers. Intentional or not, that mind-set embraces a long decline. A different approach is needed.

Instead of prioritizing maintenance based on condition or age, cities must prioritize based on financial productivity. They need to stabilize their centers of wealth by taking care of them. Any list of priorities must start with the most urgent needs of high-productivity neighborhoods and proceed through all the current needs of those places before moving on to other parts of town.

Mow the grass. Sweep the streets. Patch the sidewalks. Pick up the trash. Fill the potholes. These are the urgent needs that need to be prioritized.

I'm not suggesting – as many professional city staff would be inclined to believe – that maintenance means big, transformative projects. That is what maintenance has come to mean: large projects built all at once to a finished state with efficiency as the value elevated above all others. What results is a short period where everything looks nice followed by a long period of decline that ends in an extended, sometimes permanent, state of dilapidation.

No, I'm describing maintenance that is more like the way the Walt Disney Corporation maintains their theme parks: ongoing basic maintenance with an obsessive attention to detail.

See a streetlight out: replace it. See a weed: pull it. See a cross-walk faded: repaint it. See a sidewalk broken: fix it. The neighborhoods that are generating such wealth for the community need to be showered with love.

Doing so is not only the most sensible thing a financially strapped community can do, but it sends a strategically important signal, as well. Neighborhoods that suffer from a lack of maintenance also often suffer from a lack of confidence.

I've gotten to know Paul Stewart, the executive director of the Oswego Renaissance Association in upstate New York, and the amazing work his organization has done to stabilize, and start to revitalize, housing in Oswego's troubled neighborhoods. They do miracles with a tiny budget by focusing on projects that restore confidence. I interviewed him on the *Strong Towns Podcast* and he described the effect in this way:

> Some crisis happened long ago. Some jobs were lost and people left, and people began to lose faith in their community. So, people start to think they're not going to be staying around anymore. Then your neighbor down the street decides, "I'm not going to paint my house this year because I'm not going to be here much longer." The community is going downhill.
>
> The next neighbor across the street sees what's going on and starts to question their wisdom in investing in their property and in their house or, indeed, even in our community. They start to withdraw, and each one of us starts to send a signal to the next person that we are essentially pulling out of our own neighborhoods, out of our own cities, financially but also socially.
>
> That becomes a self-perpetuating cycle, a disinvestment cycle. As people withdraw investment, conditions worsen, as conditions worsen, confidence in the housing market – confidence in your neighborhood – drops, which causes further disinvestment, which causes further erosion of confidence.
>
> It just keeps cycling. We were basically a community engaged in a bank run on confidence. We have the capacity to revitalize our neighborhoods and communities, but we just don't have the confidence.[1]

In my hometown, our poorest neighborhoods are also some of our most financially productive. There is a general sense among some of the more affluent in town that the people in these poor neighborhoods don't want nice things. That they don't share our values and therefore they don't put any effort into maintaining their homes or their yards. They are somehow different, even lesser, then the rest of us.

I recognize that the housing throughout these poor neighborhoods needs improvement and many of the yards lack basic maintenance, but I reject the notion that it is because the people there are fundamentally different. They seem highly rational to me. After all, why would someone invest time and money repainting their house, or fixing their roof, or mowing their yard, if it is not going to translate into an improvement in property value?

If the neighborhood is in terminal decline, and the local government has prioritized go-for-broke projects, ribbon cuttings, and shiny developments over basic neighborhood maintenance, why would someone fight that? The people in these neighborhoods aren't dumb; they are highly rational.

When a community obsesses over maintenance in a high-productivity neighborhood, they not only make a wise financial investment with public dollars, they give the neighbors the confidence to take their own energy and resources off the sidelines and put them to work building wealth. Residents can make an investment in their own home – maybe something as simple as planting a tree – and have at least some confidence that their property won't automatically depreciate over the next year. That's huge!

A strategy of obsessive maintenance is the foundation for growing the underlying land values, a key component of reestablishing the positive feedback loop that naturally drives neighborhood revitalization.

Once the basic maintenance needs of high-productivity neighborhoods have been addressed, then move on to neighborhoods with similar physical characteristics. A value-per-acre analysis identifies the most productive types of development, but what are the neighborhoods that, with a little bit of attention, could grow into that level of productivity? It is going to be those that are similar, likely directly adjacent, to the most productive neighborhoods. Keep proceeding in this fashion until the maintenance money is gone.

Local governments that prioritize maintenance based on the age and condition of the infrastructure promise all their residents they will eventually get to them, even when that promise is untrue. It might be an easier assertion to sell to the public, but it ultimately means that less of the city will be maintained, that more of what has been built will catastrophically fail, that more people will be hurt. That is a choice, even if it's not purposefully acknowledged.

Switching to an approach that prioritizes maintenance of high-productivity neighborhoods first means that more of what has been built will ultimately be maintained. The stabilization of wealth in high-productivity neighborhoods, and the increase in wealth that comes from getting neighborhood resources off the sidelines, will give the community the capacity to expand maintenance efforts.

Even so, most North American cities are going to contract over the next three decades. That means infrastructure will fail and neighborhoods will be abandoned. I suspect that a salvage process will be developed to collect and repurpose that which retains value. Even so, there likely will be neighborhoods – affluent places that have a gated-community concept – that want to opt out of paying taxes to a local government that can't provide basic maintenance.

That's a reasonable choice. Let them go. It was a mistake for the community to bring those developments onto the public balance sheet. If you cannot provide the service – and it's likely you can't – then the only prudent thing to do is acknowledge that and allow them to make other arrangements. This feels like failure because it is; it's just the type of failure that can be learned from and not repeated instead of the type that is a financial millstone around the community's neck.

A commitment to intense, ongoing maintenance of high-productivity neighborhoods is the low-risk side of the barbell strategy. That is where nearly all the city's time and resources should be directed, where it won't be squandered but instead will solidify a stable base of wealth. There are other projects on the high-risk end of the barbell that should also receive a small bit of capital each year. Once a neighborhood is stable, these are the investments that will bring about new, productive growth.

Little Bets

For a private investor using the barbell approach, the high-risk investments that create the portfolio's upside potential are a series of little bets. An investor might pick a dozen companies, each of which has the potential to take off, but each of which also has a realistic chance of going completely bankrupt. It's impossible to know up front which are the winners, and which will fail. The strategy is to diversify the small bets in the hopes of landing a few that provide that huge gain.

Layered on top of an aggressive maintenance strategy, cities need to make many small investments throughout a neighborhood, all aimed at improving the quality of life. The goal is to nudge private capital off the sidelines by responding to the struggles of people already living there. Make their lives better and things will get better.

This involves a simple, four-step approach:

1. Humbly observe where people in the neighborhood struggle going about their daily routine.
2. Identify the next smallest thing that can be done today to address that struggle.
3. Do that thing. Do it right away.
4. Repeat the process.

Identifying where people struggle requires a humble form of public engagement. Those making these investment decisions need to literally walk in the footsteps of the people they are serving, to be present as they experience the city. Consider it product testing: to observe how people are using that which has been built.

Computer algorithms monitor how users interact with apps and websites and use that information to iteratively improve a program's interface. Programmers try different things, test them out, then keep and expand what works. We need to do the same thing in cities, to iteratively improve the interface of our human habitat.

Decision-makers must observe and, better yet, authentically experience where people struggle. This means getting out and experiencing the city with intention. Walk alongside people. Observe where they go. Humbly ask them to narrate their reaction to their environment. I've done this; the results are astounding.

I walked with a mother who was pushing a stroller in the ditch. She told me she needed to go to the grocery store, didn't have a car that day, and didn't feel safe walking along the street, so she was taking the ditch, knee-high weeds and all. I observed the well-worn path she was treading and realized this was a struggle being shared with others.

I met an elderly woman going down the street using a walker, climbing over mounds of snow left by the snowplow. She told me she had no choice but to get to the pharmacy that day. She pointed out that the street was cleared of snow but the sidewalk wasn't, so she was walking where she had to.

I ran into three kids walking through the alley on their way to school. It had rained hard the night before and so the alley was full of mud and filth. When I asked the kids why they chose the alley, they told me that their parents instructed them that people drive too fast on the streets so they should stick to the alley. The alley was deemed safer.

Each of these struggles is a lived experience, one I would not have been aware of had I not been out to observe them. More importantly, I could have convened a public meeting and asked those who showed up to list their top priorities for improving the neighborhood and it's very unlikely any of these struggles would have come up. They are the kind of thing people accept, the gradually diminishing expectations of a long decline. The high return on investment we are seeking on this end of the barbell comes primarily from reversing expectations.

This return also comes from limiting our approach to little bets. A common reaction for a local government that has identified a problem is to seek a comprehensive solution: Put large amounts of money into fixing it once and for all. A city dedicated to intensive maintenance is not going to have a large amount of money for comprehensively addressing each localized struggle. And even if it did, a large project may solve the immediate problem only to reveal that solution creates more serious and urgent problems. That's the way complex human habitat operates.

It is critical that the responses considered are the next *smallest* thing that can be done. There are a lot of improvements that can be made with paint, straw bales, and a shovel. Working at this scale – using a hacker mind-set – allows quick action. There is no need for years of study or deliberation. Little bets can be quickly undone if they don't achieve the desired results, or if they have unanticipated negative consequences.

This allows a neighborhood to iterate. We can try things and see what happens. We not only receive direct feedback on our work, but we can learn from mistakes when the cost of failure is low. This is the mechanism that smart, adaptive systems use to assemble themselves.

Most importantly, working quickly through small iterations changes the relationship between residents and those who would make change. Instead of customers who pay taxes expecting a service, people become collaborators, their actions and responses dictating the next set of public improvements.

With local government responsive to the struggles of the people in a neighborhood – instead of grant programs, big developers, or bureaucratic processes – residents gain confidence in the direction of the neighborhood. Give people confidence, and a little bit of room to be creative, and amazing things happen.

I met Mike Lydon, one of the authors of *Tactical Urbanism: Short-Term Action for Long-Term Change*, back in 2010, when his ideas for iterating rapid change were forming. I must admit, I was still doing some traditional engineering and planning work then and the stories of pallet benches, pop-up parks, and temporary crosswalks Mike shared seemed fun, but frivolous. I quickly came to recognize how wrong I was.

For a fraction of the cost of an engineering study, Mike and his team transform entire streets. Their do-it-yourself approach has unleashed a flood of creativity and initiative. I've witnessed their work and seen a block of empty storefronts transformed into a bustling economic hub, dangerous streets made passable, and empty spaces turned into wealth-radiating gathering spaces, all on a tiny hacker's budget.

These are real financial gains from very little investment, turning community assets from underperforming to wealth generating, all while improving the quality of life for people. This is how Mike and his colleague Anthony Garcia describe the process in their book, *Tactical Urbanism*.

Tactical Urbanism is frequently applied to what urban sociologist William "Holly" Whyte called the "huge reservoir of space yet untapped by imagination." Today's reservoirs – vacant lots, empty storefronts, overly wide streets, highway underpasses, surface parking lots, and other underused public spaces – remain prominent in our towns and cities and have become the targets of entrepreneurs, artists, forward-thinking government officials, and civic-minded "hacktivists." Such groups increasingly view the city as a laboratory for testing ideas in real time, and their actions have led to a variety of creative and entrepreneurial initiatives realized in the rise of food trucks, pop-up stores, better block initiatives, chair bombing, parklets, shipping container markets, do-it-yourself (DIY) bike lanes, guerrilla gardens, and other hallmarks of the Tactical Urbanism movement.[2]

None of these projects were the result of a master plan, the formal process cities go through to envision change. Instead, these quick and responsive hacks create changes that can actually be experienced – not just imagined – by the people they impact, a way more powerful approach to making change.

The related work of Jason Roberts and the Better Block Foundation is similarly inspirational. Jason, a website designer from the Oak Cliff neighborhood of Dallas with no technical experience in city-building, started doing projects to transform entire blocks as a demonstration of what was possible. He told me that they started with the Dallas book of codes and "tried to see how many we can break."

Of course, this was not done in pursuit of deviancy. Quite the opposite. Jason would invite city council members to witness the temporary neighborhood transformation – bikes lanes, street trees, shops open for business, street art, music – and ask them if they liked it. With dozens of smiling constituents milling around enjoying things, the public officials would always voice their enthusiasm. This is when Jason would give them a list of the rules they were breaking, the regulations preventing the transformation from becoming permanent.

The Better Block Foundation now travels to cities helping train local leaders – both inside and outside of government – to make these iterative changes themselves. They developed an entire open-source catalog of hacks and improvements and made it available at betterblock.org. Together with the Tactical Urbanism toolbox, these are proven models for incremental approaches local leaders can use to make high-returning investments in any neighborhood.

The keys to making this work are to take cues from an observation of where people struggle, seek to respond quickly to address those struggles, observe the reaction, and continue to repeat. With little bets, we're not seeking a solution; we're humbly iterating responses to cultivate a wealthier and more prosperous place.

Maintenance secures a community's wealth; little bets are how to expand it.

Filling in the Gaps

The "reservoirs untapped by imagination" are everywhere in our cities. In fact, for the typical American city, the amount of underutilized space is mind-numbing. Most Americans don't experience it because they interface with human habitat through the windshield of an automobile. The empty space is difficult to perceive when speeding past at 15 to 30 times the speed our ancestors would have experienced. Get out and walk, however, and the number and size of the gaps are overwhelming.

All that space – the space between buildings, all the buffers and ditches, all the parking lots and redundant access roads – represents nonperforming assets costing the community enormous sums of money while producing next to nothing in return. When we thought we were rich, or were going to become rich, we skipped over these places, not bothering to consider the return on our public investment. Now that we know better, we need to go back and find ways to make use of this space.

Planners often call this process *infill*, but I intentionally don't use that term. Modern infill projects are done with the same destructive mind-set that has undermined the financial health of our cities: that new development should be done in large increments and built to a finished state. Very little – almost nothing – in our cities can ever be built to a finished state, and so each of these gaps represents an opportunity to establish the first increment of the development process.

Monte Anderson, an incremental developer with Options Real Estate in Duncanville, Texas, told me once that the first increment of commercial development was a tent. Monte has rehabilitated entire neighborhoods and I thought he was kidding, until I started noticing what was right in front of me.

Street venders – tents! – the true first iteration of commercial development.

The city of Muskegon, Michigan, took this to the next iteration by installing an entire block of what are essentially storage sheds on an empty lot near their downtown. They did a minimal amount of work to bring in some sand and plastic patio furniture to turn a vacant lot into a temporary park. They then added the sheds along the street to fill a gap in the commercial streetscape, connecting their farmers market to the downtown. The sheds are rented out at affordable rates to startup businesses, several of which proved so successful that they have graduated to larger spots in the downtown.

Muskegon won the 2018 Strongest Town competition and so I was fortunate to spend a day with the mayor, Stephen Gawron, who shared the community's vision for the site. The storage sheds are temporary; when the city identifies a developer with the right vision for the city-owned vacant lot, the sheds will be moved to another location, someplace that needs a boost. In the meantime, they are a little bet that is paying off.

Joe Minicozzi's team at Urban3 has assembled some stunning data on the financial productivity of small commercial spaces. One of my favorites – and quite representative of the norm – is from High Point, North Carolina, where Joe and I were invited to make a presentation. High Point has a Walmart and a Kmart, both newer big-box stores out on edge of the city. With varying degrees of subsidy, the city and state had installed, and assumed the long-term responsibility for, tens of millions of dollars of infrastructure to make those stores possible.

In contrast, the downtown has a small restaurant called Jimmy's Pizza. It is the quintessential startup building: a nondescript, single-story, concrete block box on a narrow lot with a retail window and a front door. Every city with a traditional neighborhood has some of these. For pre-Depression development, buildings like Jimmy's Pizza were the first permanent increment of development.

A building the size of Jimmy's Pizza would fit into many of the gaps we are seeking to fill. If cities spent the next 30 years simply working to accomplish that, the resulting wealth would be enormous. Here's the value per acre of these three sites in High Point:

Walmart: $968,000/acre
Kmart: $385,000/acre
Jimmy's Pizza: $3,450,000/acre

Jimmy's Pizza is 350% more financially productive than the Walmart. It's 900% more productive than the Kmart. It uses very little of the community's resources, it generates only a small amount of liability, yet it makes fantastic use of its space. And it's a marginal building in a neglected neighborhood; imagine what would happen to the wealth here if the neighborhood were improving, not declining.

The financial success of Jimmy's Pizza is about more than just the wealth created on the site. When cities start to fill in the gaps with startup buildings like this, they change the entre-preneurial culture of the community. The profits from Jimmy's Pizza go, of course, to Jimmy. And Jimmy is important to the community because he's fully vested. It's people like Jimmy who attend the local church, put their kids in local schools, volunteer on the parent-teacher board, sponsor a youth softball team, and put a float in the Independence Day parade.

Small business owners like Jimmy put their money in local banks. They use the services of local accountants and attorneys. They advertise in the struggling local paper. They use a local ad agency. In short, unlike the big-box stores, they are part of a local economic ecosystem, one that passes capital around within the community before that wealth escapes outside. To build wealth, communities need to cultivate this kind of ecosystem.

Allowing residential neighborhoods the same kind of startup opportunity is critical to building successful economic ecosystems. Again, planning language often gets in the way. Planners like to describe neighborhoods with both homes and neighborhood-friendly businesses as *mixed use*. Our ancestors would have simply called them *neighborhoods*. Little has done more to atrophy our neighborhoods than the planning profession's fixation on a building's use instead of its architecture, style, or form.

Likewise, planners often refer to single-family homes that are less than 1,000 square feet as "tiny homes." Again, these were just "homes" to the people who came before us. In neighborhoods that evolve over time, starting small and incrementally growing was a way to build wealth, for a family and the community. When city regulations demand that everything be built at a large scale and to a finished state, we not only price out much of society but we ensure that many of those who do own a home will struggle with that investment.

It is critical that every neighborhood in America be allowed, by right, to evolve to the next level of development intensity. That means empty spaces need to be allowed starter homes, even small houses, on footprints that can be expanded over time. It also means that single-family homes must be allowed to add accessory apartments, or convert to a duplex, without any special permitting, approval of neighbors, or added conditions. To become more financially productive, we need our neighborhoods to thicken up.

Allowing all neighborhoods to evolve to the next increment of intensity is essential to creating positive feedback loops. No neighborhood can be kept under glass, prevented from changing over time, without doing damage to the entire community. Stagnant, frozen neighborhoods are the deepest dysfunction the post-war development experiment has created.

Even so, the next increment of development must be allowed by right, but no more. Neighborhoods need to evolve, but I'm now going to make the case for some prudent constraints on that growth.

Prudent Constraints

In pre-Depression development patterns, there were natural constraints on our capacity to transform neighborhoods. The main limiting factor was mechanical: We knew how to build skyscrapers, but we lacked the machinery to make that happen at scale. We also had constraints with everything from mobilizing capital to the capacity of heating and cooling equipment in different environments.

Going back even further in history, to times before the widespread use of elevators, there was a natural height limit to most buildings. Two and three stories were comfortable. Buildings as high as six stories would often be built in the most valuable places. Going taller meant walking up many more flights of stairs than could be routinely justified, a natural limit on development intensity.

These natural limitations created an equilibrium between the forces of incremental outward expansion of cities and the forces that incrementally intensified existing development. The first European city I ever flew into was Milan. On approach, the pilot announced that the city could be seen out the window. I looked but didn't see it because I was looking for the skyscrapers that a North American city of 1.4 million would have. There might be buildings taller than six stories in Milan, but I didn't see one.

San Diego has roughly 1.4 million people, as well. In contrast to Milan, there are hundreds of buildings greater than six stories in San Diego. I've been there many times and I've found the development pattern confusing to the point of being disorienting. The pockets of intense investments follow no discernible pattern.

It is a common experience in San Diego for a street to have a series of one- and two-story buildings, then a 20-story tower, then go back to one- and two-story buildings. In a world where there is a rational relationship between the value of the land and the value of the improvement on that land, this kind of random pattern should never happen.

That it is common in San Diego and other major cities suggests one of three things. Either, first, whoever built the tower is a fool for building something so overvalued on land so lacking in value. Or, second, the underlying land is so valuable that all those one- and two-story buildings are soon to be redeveloped. Or, third, there is something deeply broken in the relationship between the value of the land and the value of what is built on it.

In the case of San Diego – and many cities in North America – it is the third explanation I find most compelling. Developers can be induced to do many dumb things, but they will not repeatedly overbuild on cheap land. The land *has* tremendous value. The reason the one- and two-story buildings aren't redeveloping isn't demand; it is due to the way the properties are regulated. There are a unique set of incentives that is inducing cities like San Diego to evolve in ways different than Milan, to end up with random jumps of intensity instead of smoother increments of change.

Consider three adjacent parcels of identical size, shape, and all other defining characteristics. One contains a single-family home worth $200,000. The second is a vacant lot. The third parcel contains a 12-story condominium unit worth $10 million. If the vacant lot in the middle is put up for sale, what should the asking price be (Figure 8.2)?

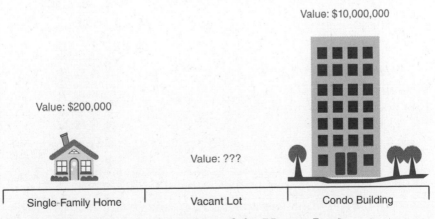

Figure 8.2 What Is the Value of the Vacant Lot?

The most logical way to make that determination is to look at the adjacent properties and determine how the parcel could be developed. What is its highest and best use?

If the purchaser of the parcel was going to build a single-family home consistent with the local market, they could pay up to 15% of the final sale price of $200,000 – or $30,000 – for the vacant lot and still make the math work. However, if the plan is to build a $10 million condo unit, the purchaser could pay 50 times that much, about $1.5 million.

If you owned the vacant lot, would you rather have $30,000 or $1.5 million? The answer is obvious.

Now that we've established the value of the vacant lot, look again at the value of the single-family home (Figure 8.3). The underlying land is the same as the vacant lot, and if it really were worth $200,000, even with the price of demolishing the home, that would be comparative steal.

That's why it's not worth $200,000. It's worth far more, simply because of the development potential.

There are some fantastic breakdowns in market feedback here. The main one is that, for San Diego to develop an entire city of multi-story condo units at the intensity suggested by the

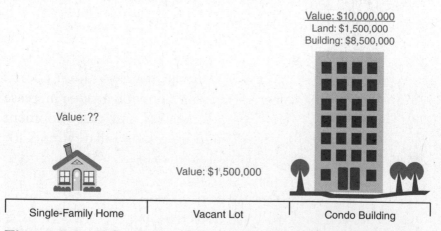

Value: ??

Value: $1,500,000

Value: $10,000,000
Land: $1,500,000
Building: $8,500,000

Single-Family Home   Vacant Lot   Condo Building

Figure 8.3 What Is the Value of the Single-Family Home?

underlying land values, the city would need tens of millions of new people. That's not going to happen, so prices should drop.

They don't, and that's because the next increment of development is not allowed. Or, where it is allowed, it has nearly as cumbersome a regulatory process, with as much uncertainty, as a more intensive development. Neighbors are given outsized influence to stop change. Environmental regulations call for extensive reviews. Various boards and commissions all get their say, even for modest projects.

That means the only developers who can pay the price and build are ones with the capacity to work through years of regulatory process, despite the uncertainty, or the ones who have special insider knowledge, or those who have both. In any case, the resulting projects are going to be large. And seemingly randomly located.

This reality has the pernicious side effect of stagnating otherwise perfectly fine neighborhoods. Some are "protected" from development with restrictive zoning, regulations that try and keep the neighborhood in an artificial stasis. This can create a temporary state of prosperity, especially when the neighborhood is disproportionately affluent. As soon as the affluence, and corresponding political influence, begin to wane, the neighborhood becomes the target of random intensity leaps by savvy and connected developers.

Other neighborhoods become trapped in decline. With the bulk of the overall property value being inflated land prices, there is little incentive to make any improvements to the property. Adding a new roof, for example, won't provide a value increase if the property is priced for a scrape off and redevelopment scenario. The poorest people wind up paying inflated rents for low-quality housing in neighborhoods where they can't afford to own. And, if things ever turn around, they will be quickly priced out and forced to move.

I could add to these distortions the centralized mechanisms of finance that induce larger developments, the national building and fire codes that favor massive new construction projects over incremental expansion, or the environmental rules that apply more scrutiny to neighborhood redevelopment than nature-wrecking projects out on the edge, among a long list of things we've done to make incremental development exceedingly difficult.

Much of this our cities have no direct control over, but the key parts they do. To remove as many distortions as possible, to give neighborhoods a chance to evolve, to build wealth in neighborhoods that is not merely transactional but reflected in the net worth of the people living there, cities must allow, by right, the next increment of intensity throughout all neighborhoods, and they must limit by-right development to only the next increment.

The goal is to thicken up neighborhoods, to create feedback loops that allow emergent prosperity to build on itself. No neighborhood can be exempt from change, but no neighborhood should experience radical change all at once. This is the prudent discipline we must impose on ourselves.

Complex systems overwhelmed with resources stop behaving in complex ways. They become merely complicated, losing the feedback mechanisms that drive adaptation. The temptation to work only in bold ways, to embrace instant and comprehensive transformation as a strategy, guarantees eventual atrophy and decline. If our cities are to be truly strong, they must resist the easy path and dedicate themselves to the work.

Cities can and should grow rapidly where that option is available to them, but that growth needs to be one step at a time, not huge leaps in the dark.

Suburban Retrofit

I'm going to use the remaining space in this chapter to discuss the concept of "Suburban Retrofit," which is also sometimes called "Sprawl Repair." Some very brilliant people have looked at failing suburban developments and, given the modern approach to development (build in large blocks, to a finished state), come up with a way to reimagine old sites for new uses.

It is hard to overstate how creative and architecturally impressive this work is. One schematic I saw took a failed big-box store site and started by running a street down the middle to create a walkable Main Street. The parking lot was then transformed into an adjacent urban village with lots of housing, parks, and open space. It was idyllic.

Another design I reviewed retrofitted a neighborhood of single-family homes on cul-de-sacs. The first step was to connect the streets to form a grid. Then the intersections were intensified with commercial buildings. In between these commercial centers, the residential homes were reconstructed to bring them up to the street and form a more walkable environment. Again, as an exercise in design, it was gorgeous.

I have serious doubts about the capacity of Americans to experience Suburban Retrofit as anything more than a niche undertaking in the most affluent places. The cost of these projects is enormous, far beyond what makes sense for most places. The number of people and businesses it would take to make a big-box store on the edge of town viable is more than most communities have to spare.

And, if Suburban Retrofit of a site is successful, then there is an oasis of prosperity amid a disconnected suburban landscape, something that seems to merely repeat the mistakes of the modern development approach.

Many technical professionals who advise cities, along with many developers well versed in both subsidies and municipal desperation, are smitten by the concept of Suburban Retrofit. It allows them to pretend that their bold visions can lead the way out of the decline we're trapped in.

Our cities have had their fill of bold visions. It's now time for an extended period of humility.

Notes

1. "Paul Stewart on Neighborhood Revitalization", *Strong Towns Podcast*, September 8, 2016.
2. Mike Lydon and Anthony Garcia, *Tactical Urbanism, Short-Term Action for Long-Term Change* (Washington, DC: Island Press, 2015).

9

Place-Oriented Government

There was skepticism in the room when I finished a presentation to a group of city managers in Mississippi. These are the unelected professionals appointed to manage the day-to day affairs of cities. They were not impressed with the engineer from Minnesota.

I told them that their cities were insolvent, that they were making bad capital investments, and that they needed to change their approach to growth and development if they wanted to get out of the financial hole they were in. I had shown them the math – all the data and charts – but they weren't buying it.

One of these city leaders took issue with the entire narrative. In a deep Southern drawl, he argued that he and his colleagues were good stewards of the taxpayers' money. He suggested that the capital projects they had done all followed accepted practice and had a positive return on investment. He was quite assertive, and very insistent.

I tried a different approach. I offered that, if these were such great investments, if they all paid solid returns, instead of borrowing the money or raising taxes, they could redirect their pension funds as a source of capital. Then their pension funds could capture the great returns from their wise management. It was a way for them to have skin in the game, to align their own future with that of the communities they serve.

The room went quiet for a moment, then exploded with laughter. The city managers slapped each other on the back and nodded enthusiastically. *You mean that kind of return.* There wasn't one of them willing to use their pension funds in that way, and everyone in the room knew it. I had made my point and we now understood each other.

The Local Government Response to Hardship

I've been in the private sector my entire professional career and I've heard all the jokes – some of them quite hilarious – about government employees. Like all good humor, there is some factual basis for critique, but I've not found the stereotype of the incompetent government bureaucrat – biding their time, filling out forms, going to meetings – to be based on reality.

This is especially true for city government, specifically among the professional leadership. Running a municipal corporation is demanding, as difficult if not more so than most private-sector undertakings. The culture is different, of course, and the values emphasized diverge, but my experience working with organizations big and small has shown that the distribution of competence (and incompetence) throughout an organization is fairly consistent, regardless of whether it is a public- or private-sector undertaking.

Where private and public sectors differ the most is in their response to feedback, particularly hardship. When private-sector enterprises are stressed financially, they tend to cut staff and retain programs. The reality of the private sector is that, without people willing to pay for goods or services, employees are a liability. If the organization can't bring in sufficient revenue, it will cease to exist. Tightening organizational slack will limit the kind of innovation that comes from excess resources, but cutting staff has its own way of revealing inefficiencies and driving adaptation. The company that waits too long to cut staff in a downturn might not make it through.

For the public sector, the response is very different. Local governments experiencing shortfalls might freeze hiring, but they generally find it more expedient to cut programs instead of people. The government can't fail in the same sense as a private-sector business; it can fail in its duties, but it won't go away or cease to exist. Revenues will continue to come in and so, whatever shortfalls occur, local governments have an internal incentive to prioritize their own staff. The cuts that happen instead result in more deferred maintenance, slower response times, and, worse service.

Over multiple business cycles, these diverging responses to hardship result in local governments full of legacy programs – things they've always done and just never stopped doing – and, subsequently, short on both resources and the capacity to innovate. Again, this is not because the people lack competence or motivation – I have found some of the most competent and heroic people working for local government – but because of the nature of the feedback local governments receive.

In the private sector, the price paid for keeping excess employees during a downturn is potentially enormous. For local governments, the price paid can also be enormous, but it's experienced disproportionately by the residents of the community, not the senior leadership of the local government.

This is an important distinction to understand because cities need to intentionally reorient themselves to experience more direct feedback, particularly hardship. They need to focus away from the hierarchy of governments and toward a shared experience with their own residents. Harmonizing competing interests in an infinite game of building human habitat requires local government leadership to become acutely aware of, and responsive to, the hardships experienced by people within the community.

Designed for Efficiency

Today's local governments are organized based on the efficiency model popular in business schools of the 1950s and 1960s. Borrowing much from the military, this model organizes personnel into silos based on tasks. Within each silo, a hierarchy is established with a clear chain-of-command. All of this is overseen by elected leadership, which – theoretically – directs this machine of efficiency to address community priorities.

Some may bristle at my characterization of local government as efficient, yet that is what this approach is designed to be. The primary purpose of this structure is to replicate a set of directions over and over. For the Army, it's used to direct troops across terrain to gain and occupy territory. For local government, it is set up to replicate and maintain the pattern of development used to grow the economy starting after World War II.

Consider a block of streets. The streets department will handle the design and construction of the pavement surface, sidewalks, and drainage systems. A separate utility department – with its own staff and hierarchy – will handle the underground utilities. A maintenance department will plow the snow, mow the boulevards, and fill the potholes. Parks staff will put in the street trees and shrubs. The zoning department will handle the regulations for adjacent development conforming to a plan put together by the planning department. The housing department will work on any housing issues on the properties aligning the street while the economic development department will deal with any business development issues. Public safety departments will respond to emergencies, but their operations will remain isolated from other parts of the city. All of this is coordinated and supported by an administrative staff.

It's set up this way to be efficient. The streets people might coordinate with the parks people, but they don't have to understand what the parks people do. It's a different silo; streets handles their duties and parks handles theirs. Guidance can be efficiently sent down each hierarchy to be executed. Each silo can develop their own internal expertise, culture, and champions.

While this approach is efficient, it lacks adaptability. Once a silo and hierarchy system is established, there is internal inertia that resists change. Repeated business cycles have forced most of the private sector – any part that relies on innovation – to address this shortcoming, largely by reorganizing into a flatter, team structure. Local government, with its different response to stress, has largely resisted this kind of realignment.

Some local governments have adopted a team approach for major projects, but the teams are subordinate to the silo structure and the relative hierarchy of each silo remains. The values of the department with the largest budget tend to dominate. For example, a street reconstruction project is more likely to prioritize moving traffic instead of building wealth by adding street trees because the engineering department has a much larger budget, and thus far greater clout, than the parks department.

Local governments are under constant stress to do more with less. With programs short of funding, staff priorities shift toward work that produces cash. Lots of time and energy is spent seeking grants and other funding from the federal and state governments. Many staff will commit senior resources to lobbying legislators and building relationships with those who can bring in new revenue. Others will work with large developers to bring in outside capital for new projects while generating fees for the city.

Local governments are predisposed to be internally focused on their own systems. They are highly responsive up the government food chain, adapting to available revenue streams by shifting priorities to projects that can receive state and federal funding. They are also highly responsive to businesses and developers from outside the community, who are viewed as having the capacity to bring new resources to the table.

Where local governments focus on the residents of the community, it is most often in the context of considering them customers whose needs and expectations are to be satisfied in a cheerful manner, instead of collaborators in a joint project known as the city.

This might have all made sense at a time when America's cities were merely attempting to replicate a fixed model of development. It's the wrong system for cities whose objective is to build wealth. Cities that are going to make productive use of what they have already invested in need flexibility, nuance, and – most critically – a culture that embraces early failures as a learning mechanism.

Local government needs to be reimagined, beginning with new values and objectives.

A Focus on Broad Wealth Creation

Growth is the unifying objective within modern local governments. All silos and hierarchies can align themselves around the pursuit of growth and thereby meet the priorities – directly or indirectly – of senior leadership and the broader community. Many a bad idea has been pursued without pause because it contained the hope of new growth.

Growth is an old economy objective. For local governments seeking to create successful human habitat, the centrally orienting objective needs to shift to wealth creation. Broad-based wealth creation. Cities must sacrifice growth to build stability, to close the gap between private wealth and long-term public liabilities.

This new approach requires cities to be flatter, more flexible, and increasingly strategic in their actions. They need to be able to do small projects, to iterate collaboratively and embrace failure as a learning mechanism. They must add value to routine maintenance and facilitate the next increment of maturing with a minimal amount of friction.

This doesn't mean less local government. In fact, a collaborative approach, one that takes its cues from a humble observation of where people struggle, is labor intensive. A city pursuing growth as a commodity will value the lowest possible cost in all its activities, but a city focused on building wealth pays extra for the creation of value.

Table 9.1 offers a sample of how the core priorities of a city must change to support a new approach of building wealth.

Table 9.1 How a City's Priorities Must Shift to Build Wealth

Department	Conventional Priorities	Strong Towns Priorities
City Engineer	Reducing congestion.	Building measurable wealth with each project.
	Moving automobiles quickly.	Providing an abundance of mobility options within the city.
	Securing state and federal funding to build new stuff.	Working to have a tax base sufficient to support ongoing maintenance obligations.
City Planner	Enforcing regulations.	Facilitating the next increment of maturing.
	Ensuring adequate parking.	Ensuring adequate tax base.
	Separating uses and reducing nuisances.	Ensuring new buildings fit with the neighborhood pattern.
	Projecting future growth and making plans to handle it.	Implementing adaptable systems that will respond to changing market conditions.
	Zoning.	Urban design.

(continued)

Table 9.1 How a City's Priorities Must Shift to Build Wealth (*cont'd*)

Department	Conventional Priorities	Strong Towns Priorities
Economic Development	Recruiting one business that adds 50 new jobs.	Helping 50 existing businesses add one new job each.
	Handing out subsidies to new businesses.	Reducing the burdens on existing businesses.
	Creating jobs.	Creating an environment that promotes job creation.
	Economic hunting.	Economic gardening.
Parks	Building new park facilities.	Leveraging existing parks to improve the value of surrounding properties.
	Creating a parking lot to attract more users.	Creating more walking and biking connections to serve nearby users.
	Soliciting federal grants.	Creating opportunities for locals to financially support your efforts.
	Building things that are easy to maintain.	Building things that are worth maintaining.
Housing Authority	Building affordable housing.	Ensuring that affordable housing is easy to build everywhere.
	Financing an apartment building with 20 affordable units.	Helping 20 property owners each build one accessory apartment.
	Fighting blight.	Restoring confidence.
Transit Coordinator	Serving corridors.	Connecting productive places.
	Serving only the disadvantaged.	Serving everyone.
	Covering a large area.	Providing frequent and reliable service.

Department	Conventional Priorities	Strong Towns Priorities
	Making transformative improvements as a catalyst for growth.	Scaling transit to the current level of development. Maturing transit along with the neighborhood.
	Appling for federal grants to make large improvements.	Using the resources available today to get things going.
Public Safety	Designing city to match the desired equipment.	Acquiring equipment to match the desired city.
	Decreasing response time.	Preventing collisions.
	Growing the service area.	Improving service to core neighborhoods.
	Stopping any initiative that might have safety implications (i.e., "You can't do this because . . .").	Mitigating safety implications of proposed initiatives (i.e., "To make this safe we will need to . . .").
Maintenance	Ensuring the city is easy to maintain.	Ensuring the city is worth maintaining.

These shifts in thinking are critical, but they won't happen without intentional restructuring, starting with an effort to break down silos. Project teams are an excellent way to start this process. For cities seeking to build wealth, no project can be one-dimensional. Assigning projects to a team of equal professionals with the common directive to "add value and grow the community's wealth" is better than simply giving a project to one department to complete and then allowing others to comment.

In fact, I would recommend putting a nontechnical person in charge of managing the team during the project development phase. This is the part of the project where values and priorities are asserted. It's too easy for technical people to elevate their own area of expertise to the highest priority; after all, they understand it deeply, having often sacrificed the pursuit of more general knowledge in order to build specialized expertise. Technical people are helpful, but not in conceptualizing complex human habitat.

Over time, the structure of local government must shift from hierarchical silos based on areas of expertise to geographically focused teams employing people with a broad range of abilities. These teams should be evaluated based on the success of their focus area, particularly in building wealth. No more accolades for people who merely perform transactions, such as permits issued, subsidies given, or miles of roadway constructed.

Celebrate Maintenance

If the community is going to have a commitment to intense, ongoing maintenance of high-productivity neighborhoods, it must celebrate the people who lead that effort. To the extent that local governments celebrate anyone today, it's generally the person who brings in the big project, gets the large grant, or delivers on some expansion undertaking. There is something cultural about this we must intentionally struggle against.

Consider an organization having three projects requiring equally technical skill sets. Project #1 is high profile. If it goes well, there will be a lot of handshakes, photo opportunities, and awards. If it doesn't, it will make everyone involved look bad, but the organization will still be okay. Project #2 is routine but still in the public eye. If it goes well, there won't be a lot of accolades, but if it goes poorly, it will really damage the organization's credibility. Project #3 is mundane to the extreme. If all goes well, nobody will even be aware it was done, but if it should go wrong, it will destroy the organization along with all pensions, equity, and legacy value.

Which project does the best project manager get assigned to? Which of the three is assigned to the worst?

Let me ask another way: Which project does the best project manager want to work on? What project does the least influential project manager get stuck with?

Project #1 is going to attract the highest performers. Project #2 is going to appeal to those who aspire to climb the organizational hierarchy, but need the experience or resume to shift into that top tier. In a three-person competition, the mundane task without the accolades goes to the lowest performer.

That might work in a private company where management takes calculated risks each day, but what if we're in the public sector? And what if, in the infinite game cities are playing, failure on the mundane project means damage to property, dislocation of people, expensive emergency repairs, and potentially even loss of human life? Or what if it merely means the slow decline of the systems the community has built or the ongoing denuding of the community's wealth and prosperity? We need our best people leading the charge on maintenance.

None of this is to suggest that there aren't smart people currently working on maintenance but more of an observation that these people toil in the trenches in obscurity with little appreciation – let alone acclaim – for their efforts. That is, until something goes wrong.

This is a systematic problem. I worked with someone who maintained sewage pumps for a city. He consistently received high marks from the state oversight organization and numerous "Operator of the Year" awards. The problem is, he completely faked the data he submitted – he wasn't doing the work – something anyone could have figured out with five minutes on a spreadsheet (I had). He was managing a critical system, the failure of which was not only costly but could have had serious environmental impacts. The job was mundane, a low priority despite its importance, so it was given to someone willing to work cheap and given little real oversight.

Can cities find a way to elevate the people who do these tasks day in and day out, whose seriousness over the long-term threats of failure are not dulled by their infrequent occurrence? I'm not sure, but at the city level, we need to get these people out of the obscure back rooms and make them part of our day-to-day conversations. We need to have them at the table so their voices are not passed through the filter of people with other ambitions and priorities. We need to celebrate the people who do maintenance, pay them more, and give their positions more prestige within our cultural conversation.

Every local government has systems that fall into one of three categories:

1. Critical: Something goes bad and it takes the whole thing down.
2. Redundant: Critical systems that have backups and alternatives in place.
3. Noncritical: Something goes bad and only a small area is impacted.

These systems can further be categorized as maintenance intensive or low maintenance.

Every city should have a list of critical systems. The odds are, any critical system with lots of required maintenance is already getting attention. It's likely the highest-performing people are already assigned to them and given some degree of prestige. There are probably even efforts to find ways to add redundancies so the systems are not critical. That's great management.

It's the "critical–low maintenance" systems that come to our attention at the wrong time. This is the seawall in New Orleans, the spillway at the Oroville dam, the main lift pump on the city's sewage collection system. We need them to work – they're critical – but we can go decades, or even lifetimes, without suffering any consequence for their neglect. Local leadership needs to be intentional about making these systems front and center, and not allowing them to become an afterthought. This is where management – top administration and elected officials – need to shower their attention and overcome the natural tendency to have these systems fade into the background.

Considering a new set of priorities for building wealth, cities also need to give fresh evaluation of what is critical and what is not. For example, it snows a lot where I live in Minnesota. We've culturally prioritized clearing the snow from the streets and consider that a critical function of government. We don't worry about most sidewalks for 48 hours and, even then, it's an enforcement matter; the city expects private homeowners to clear the sidewalks.

If we're trying to increase the financial productivity of our neighborhoods, get private capital off the sidelines, and work to incrementally build wealth, we need to recognize that sidewalk maintenance is critical for many people. Many have one way of getting around – walking – and if clearing the sidewalk is a distant, subordinate, maintenance objective to having every street cleared for automobile traffic, it's not going to create the needed level of confidence in the neighborhood.

If maintenance is the priority – and it must be the priority – then the people who perform maintenance must be a priority. That's a different culture, one where the maintenance worker is a value-adding artisan, not the lowest-cost cog in a bigger system.

Recognizing Our Confirmation Bias

During World War II, islands in the South Pacific that had little prior contact with Japanese or American/European explorers were subjected to a series of war-related occupations. Troops would come in and set up landing strips along with all the other associated infrastructure – barracks, offices, control towers, and so on – and, in the process, share some of their stores with the natives on the island. In many cases, the stuff that was shared proved lavish for people who had been used to lives of privation.

Then the war ended, the troops left, and, of course, the materials ceased coming. How would the residents of these islands restore the level of abundance they had experienced? You can imagine a local leader and their *Make Melanesia Great Again* campaign. All we need to do – or so it goes – is to do what was done before and we'll get the same results. It's so obvious, it's hardly even debatable.

The Pacific Islanders set about recreating the conditions that they witnessed bringing about the largess. They cleared straight paths through the forest for airplanes to land on. They built model airplanes out of grass and sticks and parked them near the runway. They erected control towers and placed people in them to sit for hours with mock-headphones they had carved out of wood. They dressed like soldiers, paraded around, and even sat in mock meetings. They believed that if they did these things – the things they had witnessed others do – the planes full of cargo would start landing again.

Of course, since we understand manufacturing, industrial agriculture, metal working, supply chains, and the logistics of shipping, we grasp the simplicity of their understanding. We call these people primitive, even backward, in their logic. Yet this behavior is something we mimic.

It's hard to even estimate how many cities I've been in where, in a meeting with local leaders, a dignitary, or some advocacy group, a plan is put forth for action based on the simple observations of what worked in another place. For example, we witness a city with a vibrant downtown, notice they have decorative lighting, and so we fixate on the logical solution to our struggling downtown being decorative lighting. Or another place where a senior apartment building met the needs of the mayor's elderly parent, so now we need a senior apartment building. In these instances, we mimic the Pacific Islanders and simplify vast complexity down to something we can understand and act upon.

This isn't a problem – in fact, it's often quite helpful – if our capacity to act on our insights is limited. We can be laughably wrong, but if we can only act on that knowledge incrementally, we'll discover our folly before we do great harm to others. The crisis comes about when our confirmation bias is fueled by large budgets, tremendous debt capacity, and a culture that rewards bold action. Then we can, and often do, confidently pursue our foolishness to great destruction.

The Pacific Islanders who built airport runways may have been simple, but they were not stupid. The same impulses that drove their brains are active in ours. We are just as likely to attribute random success to our own genius as we are to assign blame for our failures to an unforeseen event. That's illogical – they are both a byproduct of our efforts as well as a degree of randomness – but human reasoning is anything but logical.

In modern America, a local government has a dangerous capacity to blow itself up. Stripped by the state of many basic tools for managing their own affairs, cities are nevertheless allowed to take on unpayable levels of debt, unmanageable levels of infrastructure liability, and give away a generation's worth of the community's wealth. Combine this capacity with the human predilection to have unwarranted faith in our own rationality and it creates a volatile asymmetry, where decision-makers have some benefit from large public gambles, but the public is disproportionately exposed to the downside.

The Russian-roulette equation – a reasonable chance of success with a nonnegligible risk of total failure – makes no sense in an infinite game. Prudent people don't risk what they have and need for something they don't have but could live without.

And like the Pacific Islanders, the big project mentality has it backward. The Coliseum was not built in anticipation of Rome. The Eiffel Tower wasn't built before Paris. The Brooklyn Bridge was not built before decades of development in Manhattan and Brooklyn. These investments are not the catalyst for success; they are the culmination of success, a celebration of who we are and the work we have done. Table 9.2 suggests more appropriate ways of thinking when it comes to building better cities.

Table 9.2 Replacing Conventional Thinking with Strong Towns Thinking

Conventional Thinking	Strong Towns Thinking
Build it and they will come.	Get them to come so you can afford to build it.
Major projects are a catalyst for growth.	Major projects are made possible by productive growth.
Major projects create jobs.	Jobs are the natural byproduct of a productive place.
Finance major projects with debt to speculate on future growth.	Finance major projects only with a secure and stable tax base.
Future maintenance liabilities are the responsibility of future generations.	A project is only viable if it builds wealth for future generations, not unfunded obligations.

It is easier to work with simple or complicated systems than complex ones. It's easier to live in a world we pretend to understand than one where we purposefully struggle with the unknown. It is easier to design a city using our own limited vision than it is to accommodate the hopes and dreams of thousands of people we will never even meet.

This is not going to be easy. That is the burden of knowing. Accept it.

Understanding Debt

Cities that take on debt are bringing future spending into the present while obligating future residents to pay for that spending. Unlike for the federal government, where some concepts of credit cycles suggest that it's acceptable to borrow money without planning to pay it back, there are no theories of finance that allow a city to avoid a hard reckoning with its debts and obligations. For a local government, taking on debt is a serious matter.

There are legitimate ways for a local government to use debt, but like most areas of modern society where debt has become a routine matter of making ends meet, cities have become blasé about it. Local leaders who use general obligation debt to cover routine budget gaps are acting immorally, avoiding discomfort today by inviting greater pain tomorrow. Those who use revenue bonds to finance speculative private development – and then use the developer fees for cash flow – are likewise suspect. Easy credit has culturally legitimized many actions that prior generations would rightfully have considered obscene.

Local governments taking on debt to make an investment must ensure three things. First, the expenditure must have the potential to improve the city's financial position. Taking on debt for a project that provides some quality-of-life benefit today – for example, improving the flow of traffic – can only be justified when all maintenance obligations are accounted for, there is no debt, and the community broadly supports repaying the obligation in short order. You don't put in a swimming pool when your roof is leaking.

Second, the improvement in the city's financial position must be measurable in terms of dollars. It's not enough to measure saved time, reduced carbon emissions, or an improvement in happiness and equate that to dollars. An investment that justifies debt must have a real return.

Finally, cities must obsessively measure the return on investment, compare that return to the assumptions made for the project, and use that experience to inform subsequent investments. In this sense, doing projects with debt becomes an iterative learning process, part of developing a local culture of civic collaboration across generations. Cities that don't track and publicly report the return on investment for debt-funded projects are signaling that they either don't care or don't want to know.

Local governments can also legitimately take on debt for cash flow, but this tends to be the most problematic use of leverage. Too often – in fact, almost always in the instances I've experienced – a local government confuses its insolvency for merely a cash-flow problem. That is disastrous because it allows the community to put off dealing with the underlying financial problems while continuing on as if everything is fine. When debt capacity is gone and the underlying insolvency is revealed, the problems are far worse and the responses more limited.

As a way to understand the deceptive nature of cash-flow debt, consider a city that has four streets. Each street lasts four years before it needs to be repaired. One street was built each year and so they are on a nice four-year maintenance rotation. If the city is solvent – if there is enough wealth in the community where the tax revenue can cover the city's long-term obligations – then there should never be a need for debt. Each year, each street produces one-quarter of the tax revenue needed to fix the street (Figure 9.1). After four years, every street is fixed and the process starts over.

Cities don't generally have their maintenance obligations so nicely staggered. Typically, they come in bunches, an echo of the growth spurt in which they were originally built. Consider a scenario where all four streets in the example city were built in the first year. All would need maintenance at the same time four years later. In that case, the city could tax four times the normal

Scenario 1: Debt not necessary

Year 1					Year 2				
Street	Tax Revenue		Expense		Street	Tax Revenue		Expense	
1	$	0.25	$	1.00	1	$	0.25		
2	$	0.25			2	$	0.25	$	1.00
3	$	0.25			3	$	0.25		
4	$	0.25			4	$	0.25		
TOTAL	$	1.00	$	1.00	TOTAL	$	1.00	$	1.00

Year 3					Year 4				
Street	Tax Revenue		Expense		Street	Tax Revenue		Expense	
1	$	0.25			1	$	0.25		
2	$	0.25			2	$	0.25		
3	$	0.25	$	1.00	3	$	0.25		
4	$	0.25			4	$	0.25	$	1.00
TOTAL	$	1.00	$	1.00	TOTAL	$	1.00	$	1.00

Figure 9.1   Debt Is Not Necessary because Cash Flow Is Sufficient to Fund Maintenance

Scenario 2: Legitimate cash flow

Year 1				Year 2			
Street	Tax Revenue		Expense	Street	Tax Revenue		Expense
1	$	0.25	$ 4.00	1	$	0.25	
2	$	0.25		2	$	0.25	
3	$	0.25		3	$	0.25	
4	$	0.25		4	$	0.25	
TOTAL	$	1.00	$ 4.00	TOTAL	$	1.00	$ -
DEBT	$	3.00		DEBT	$	2.00	

Year 3				Year 4			
Street	Tax Revenue		Expense	Street	Tax Revenue		Expense
1	$	0.25		1	$	0.25	
2	$	0.25		2	$	0.25	
3	$	0.25		3	$	0.25	
4	$	0.25		4	$	0.25	
TOTAL	$	1.00	$ -	TOTAL	$	1.00	$ -
DEBT	$	1.00		DEBT	$	-	

Figure 9.2   Debt Is Used to Make Up for a Cash-Flow Shortfall but Revenue Is Sufficient to Pay Back the Debt before Another Round of Maintenance

amount the first year and nothing in the next three, something culturally difficult to pull off. Or, they could take on debt in the first year to fix all four streets and then pay that debt back over the next three years. That is a legitimate cash-flow problem that the local government can solve with a judicious use of debt (Figure 9.2). (Note: Obviously this is very simplified and so I've not bothered with realistic time frames or interest.)

Consider the second scenario again, but this time in a city where the tax revenue is only half of what is needed to maintain all four streets. The city is not collecting enough money from each street to cover the cost of maintenance. As in the second scenario, the city takes on debt in the first year to cover the surge in maintenance costs, but, at the end of the fourth year when the streets need to be fixed again, the first round of debt has not been paid off. Now the city has a maintenance obligation and debt, a reflection of the underlying insolvency (Figure 9.3).

Scenario 3: Confusing insolvency with cash flow

Year 1				Year 2			
Street	Tax Revenue		Expense	Street	Tax Revenue		Expense
1	$	0.13	$ 4.00	1	$	0.13	
2	$	0.13		2	$	0.13	
3	$	0.13		3	$	0.13	
4	$	0.13		4	$	0.13	
TOTAL	$	0.50	$ 4.00	TOTAL	$	0.50	$ -
DEBT	$	3.50		DEBT	$	3.00	

Year 3				Year 4			
Street	Tax Revenue		Expense	Street	Tax Revenue		Expense
1	$	0.13		1	$	0.13	
2	$	0.13		2	$	0.13	
3	$	0.13		3	$	0.13	
4	$	0.13		4	$	0.13	
TOTAL	$	0.50	$ -	TOTAL	$	0.50	$ -
DEBT	$	2.50		DEBT	$	2.00	

Figure 9.3 Revenue Is Not Sufficient to Cover Ongoing Maintenance Expense, but That Fact Is Covered Up with Debt

The third scenario is a case of confusing insolvency with a cash-flow problem. The local government believes they have a cash-flow problem – they perceive that there's plenty of wealth there, just not right now – but what they really have is an insolvency problem. They don't have the money to maintain everything they've promised to maintain. By borrowing money, they are piling more obligations on top of the unfunded liabilities they already have. This is a recipe for disaster.

The scary thing is that all cities that take on debt for infrastructure maintenance believe they have a cash-flow problem. They believe this despite not having done the analysis to determine whether this is true. The example I've given is ridiculously simplified: four streets over four years. Cities sometimes have hundreds of miles of streets with maintenance occurring over decades. A local government must be obsessively intentional, organized, and disciplined to discern its true financial status.

Most cities aren't. They want to believe they have a cash-flow problem because it is convenient, because insolvency is too difficult to fathom, especially when everyone else appears to be doing the exact same thing. Could everyone be wrong? Could we all be insolvent? These two questions probably cost me a total of six years in the intellectual wilderness as I clung to the notion that what I was seeing and measuring could not possibly be true, that a wisdom greater than mine had to be at work that I hadn't perceived.

I advocate giving local governments many more tools to work with than they have today, but I believe state governments have a responsibility to limit municipal debt. It's not something that can be left up to local leaders, ratings agencies, and the fickle nature of bond markets.

I gave a presentation to a group of bond analysts from one of the large ratings agencies. I showed them how public balance sheets didn't reflect the extent of municipal liability, that cities had unreported amounts of maintenance obligations totaling many times their reported pension shortfalls. The analysts were stunned, professed this was new to them, and asked a lot of good questions. Then they informed me that it wouldn't change anything about how they rated bonds because cities don't default on their debt – they have not defaulted en masse since the Great Depression – and that track record superseded all other considerations.

Few elected officials have any clue how much debt their community has. Much of it is hidden from the operating budget, tucked away in off-balance-sheet revenue accounts that are obscured by interfund transfers. An ideal state policy would require cities to report total debt. It would also limit the annual debt service of local governments, from all sources, to 5% of locally generated revenue, allowing that amount to climb to 10% with a community-wide referendum.

In the absence of state mandates, local governments should voluntarily discipline their reporting and spending in this way.

The temptation to solve today's problems with debt is too great, and the potential ramifications too serious, not to be extremely wary over municipal indebtedness.

Negative Knowledge

I was at a city council meeting where a resident showed up to complain about a neighbor who wasn't bringing their garbage can in quickly enough after pickup day. The guy making the complaint demanded that the city council enact an ordinance, with fines, for anyone who leaves their bin out more than 24 hours. Sympathetic council members quickly reached consensus on an entire set of regulations, fines, and routine inspections and then turned to me to see if I could put that package together for them to adopt.

Before responding to the city council, I listed a bunch of reasonable explanations for why someone might not collect their garbage can right away. Then I asked the man making the complaint whether he had spoken with his neighbor about the situation. He hadn't, of course, even though that would have taken far less time and energy – and likely been more helpful – than coming to the council meeting. He wanted the elected officials to address this discomfort for him. They were eager to be helpful.

This is not uncommon. Most city codes, policies, and practices are a reaction to a complaint, discomfort, or irregular situation. They are enacted in all earnestness by people doing their best to safeguard the community. Many were enacted so long ago, and for such obscure reasons, that nobody recalls precisely why. The only consensus today is that *bad things will happen* if they are repealed, and – more importantly – the people doing the repealing will be held to account.

If cities are going to build complex human habitat, the kind where individuals responding to feedback work collaboratively to make their place more prosperous, then local leaders need to resist the temptation to address every discomfort. More than that, there must be a concerted effort to repeal codes, policies, and bureaucratic processes, especially when they impede development at the next increment of intensity.

For complex systems, the rationale of improving through removal is described by Nassim Taleb in his book *Antifragile*.

> We know a lot more what is wrong than what is right, or, phrased according to the fragile/robust classification, negative knowledge (what is wrong, what does not work) is more robust to error than positive knowledge (what is right, what works). Knowledge grows by subtraction much more than by addition – given that what we know today might turn out to be wrong but what we know to be wrong cannot turn out to be right, at least not easily.[1]

I've recommended to city officials that they examine their regulations and identify those that, if they were ignored, would do damage to their community that could not be repaired in a decade. Keep only those rules and throw the rest out. There is so much to be done figuring out how to evolve cities to be financially productive, so many new lessons to be learned, that we should only restrict those things that can mortally wound the community.

Cities shouldn't be regulating things like temporary seating, siding finishes, or whether a building houses an attorney or an accountant. They should never mandate parking. They should obsess about how buildings address each other: that it opens onto the street, complements neighboring structures in scale and character, and respects the humans who traverse past it.

This is not a call for deregulation as much as a new approach. Many cities are replacing the use-based codes they adopted to facilitate post-war development patterns with form-based codes that come closer to dealing with issues directly related to financial productivity. These are positive changes, especially when the form-based approach allows the neighborhood to incrementally thicken up without needing any special permissions.

If we want productive investment, we also must be strategic with our regulation. For example, none of the buildings on the *Old and Blighted* block referenced in Chapter 7 have commercial sprinkler systems. Anyone looking to make improvements to one of these buildings must address this deficiency, an expense greater than the value of the building itself. There is no way the cost of a sprinkler will be recouped in a reasonable time frame, and so nothing happens. These buildings remain locked in regulatory purgatory; lack of investment ensures decline, but decline makes unprofitable the kind of investment needed to meet code.

The phasing of this relationship needs to be reversed. Instead of stopping all investment until full compliance is reached, the process should be used to bring the building into compliance over time. For example, if a new business wants to open in an old building, do an inspection and make sure that there are no imminent health threats – no frayed wires arcing over bails of straw under a gasoline drip – and, barring any urgent issues, let them open provisionally.

Six months later, once they have a sense of whether their business venture is viable, go out and document all the code deficiencies with the property. Rank them in terms of urgency. Require the business owner to put 3% of their revenue into an escrow account for addressing deficiencies, starting with the most urgent. When they are done, remove their provisional status and stop collecting the escrow.

To build a productive place, people must be able to start with nothing and, through their efforts, end up with something. When we raise the bar to entry, we not only induce decline, we ensure that many of our neighbors will be left behind. Successful communities raise the bar of prosperity without raising the entry fee.

Subsidiarity

A closing note in this chapter on what I've heard the great architect and urban planner Andres Duany call "the chicken problem": Who should decide whether a person can have backyard chickens? Who should establish those regulations, if any are even warranted?

The identification of *who* is the critical preface to the central question of backyard chickens. Who decides? Is this something that should be decided by the city council? Should this be a decision of the regional government? Should the state weigh in or should there be federal legislation regulating the proper care and treatment of backyard chickens?

Federal legislation seems absurd in this instance, and that is the point. A collection of neighbors can come to a decision on whether to have backyard chickens on their block. Whether or not they can *cordially* come to an agreement is beside the point: They have among them everything they need to have that conversation and make that decision.

In contrast, these neighbors are *not* capable of deciding where the regional rapid transit line should be located. Or what the capacity of the interstate should be. Or whether people of different races or incomes should be allowed to live in their community. They are not capable of making these decisions because each decision encompasses a higher level of complexity than backyard chickens.

In the United States today, who makes decisions is more impactful than what decision is ultimately made. It is absurd to suggest that Congress should regulate backyard chickens, but it is equally absurd to suggest that a few people in a neighborhood should have the capacity to, for example, block the construction of a regional transit line. American culture spends a lot of time debating what should be done, but hardly any time discussing who should make the decision.

The concept of who decides is enshrined in a principle called subsidiarity. I have come to understand subsidiarity through Catholic teaching, but the concept goes back much further. Here is how Wikipedia presents the idea:

> Subsidiarity is an organizing principle that matters ought to be handled by the smallest, lowest or least centralized competent authority. Political decisions should be taken at a local level if possible, rather than by a central authority. The *Oxford English Dictionary* defines subsidiarity as "the idea that a central authority should have a subsidiary function, performing only those tasks which cannot be performed effectively at a more immediate or local level."[2]

Central to the concept of subsidiarity is the act of offering assistance, as opposed to mandating a direction. A collection of neighbors may not be able to reach a decision on backyard chickens; perhaps they are all antagonistic and have difficulty talking to each other. A modern approach would have the city step in, take over the decision-making process, and make a definitive ruling on whether backyard chickens are allowed and under what circumstances.

In contrast, the practice of subsidiarity would call on the city to, at most, assist these quarreling neighbors with reaching a decision. They have the capacity to decide and so they *must* decide; that decision can't be made for them. Maybe a city staff member goes out and talks to everyone, or maybe the city convenes a meeting with a third-party. It might be easier and more expedient for the city to rule but taking from these neighbors the responsibility to make the decision robs them not only of their agency, but their capacity to be a collaborator in the project of building a successful city.

I am often approached by governors, state legislators, members of Congress, and, on a couple of occasions, even representatives from the executive branch of the federal government for my input on what they can do to follow a Strong Towns approach and build a stronger America. These interactions rarely go well because my answer – subsidiarity – is not the proactive set of policies they are seeking. For them, subsidiarity feels more like giving up. And power, once assumed, is difficult to relinquish.

State and federal officials frequently express their reluctance to turn over decision-making to local officials they view as incompetent, ignorant, or worse. They fail to recognize how turning city councils into glorified dog catchers, by simplifying their authority and degree of action, Congress and state legislatures have created the conditions where the most competent, innovative, and dynamic local leaders tend to stay away from city hall.

California is a particularly perplexing example of this. The state, through ballot initiatives and legislative action, has stripped most taxing authority away from cities, leaving only a couple of coarse and nonadaptive approaches in the municipal toolbox. Cities respond by doing the one thing that brings in significant new revenue – more horizontal expansion – and the state supports that directly through massive levels of transportation subsidy.

Then, given the environmental and social disaster of converting the open landscape to shoddy housing and, even worse, commercial development, as well as the obscene costs of the subsequent traffic congestion, the state enacts round after round of laws requiring environmental reviews, community engagement, and comprehensive planning and zoning regimes.

These laws have slowed – through by no means stopped – the worst development practices, but they also have the perverse effect of giving individuals, especially the wealthy and well connected, mechanisms for stopping nearly any development proposal. Housing in California has become brutally expensive, partially because individual neighborhoods are empowered to delay, if not altogether stop, projects that would create more housing.

In response, the California legislature has considered multiple proposals to strip local governments of decision-making authority on many building and permitting matters, further dulling any local initiative to adapt to the stresses being experienced. The trend in California is to rule on everything from

Sacramento, to only allow local governments the limited power needed to administer the policy direction set forth by the state.

That tendency is the opposite of subsidiarity. California is by no means alone in this reaction, but, being the largest state, California's efforts at centralization, the lurching from grand solution to grand solution in Sacramento, is the most visible example nationwide. I respect the motivation, but the relationship with local governments is not healthy.

Federal and state political leaders who want to advocate for a Strong Towns approach will embrace subsidiarity as a governing principle. When legislating, they will ask themselves: What is the smallest, lowest, or least-centralized level of decision-making where this issue can be competently dealt with? Who should make this decision? Extra effort should be made to assist instead of mandate, to build competence while increasing feedback and accountability.

This doesn't mean local governments will always make the right decision. In fact, I can guarantee that many will not. They'll make frustratingly stupid mistakes. Some of these will be hurtful, even offensive. Subsidiarity trades the dull and growing discomfort of a systematic decline for the acute pain of localized failure. Those who seek innovative responses to hardship must embrace that tradeoff.

My experience has made me skeptical, however, that state and federal governments will voluntarily devolve power, even in the face of declining capacity to enforce their will. By remaking local government to focus on the broad creation of wealth, local leaders will develop the capacity to assert their own competence. America needs that to happen.

Notes

1. Nassim Nicholas Taleb, *Antifragile: Things That Gain From Disorder* (New York: Random House, LLC, 2012).
2. https://en.wikipedia.org/wiki/Subsidiarity_(Catholicism)

10

An Intentional Life

My oldest daughter, Chloe, came home from her first day of kindergarten bursting with joy. Back then she was a chatty princess with a lot to say. My wife and I listened to her tell us about her day: her teacher, the new routine, all the new friends she was making. It was beautiful.

At one point she told us the important details about a new girl she met. This new friend had blonde hair (like Chloe) and blue eyes (like Chloe) and she liked the color pink (serendipitously, just like Chloe). With so much in common, they were destined to be friends. In fact, Chloe declared they were going to be best friends. The new girl's name was Holly.

It wasn't long after that we found out an important detail about Holly: She lived with her family in a home directly across the street from ours. Not down the road. Not up the block. Directly opposite the street from our home.

My wife and I had lived in our house for over a dozen years at that point. Holly's family had lived in theirs even longer. We were both active families, involved in the community, with work, and with our churches. Yet, the thick woods covering the lots we each occupied along a cul-de-sac was enough of a barrier to our getting to know each other that we didn't even realize our neighbors across the street had a little girl the same age as ours.

That is, until they met at the kindergarten in the elementary school six miles away.

I've spent a good portion of my professional life trying to understand why cities struggle financially. Why, despite all the growth, all the infrastructure, all the work that I was involved in trying to create prosperity, did the cities I knew most intimately have such profound financial problems? In searching for that answer, I have encountered questions that go far beyond my inquiry, questions I was unprepared for and feel incapable of adequately answering.

How much more joy, happiness, and love would my daughter have experienced growing up had we understood that her best friend lived a few hundred feet away? How many walks with the stroller would have been made a little more lovely with neighbors?

Questions like these are outside of my expertise, yet I've found myself dwelling on them. They are the essential questions, the ones that matter most. As I ponder what it means to be human, co-evolved with a habitat that – through thousands of years of trial and error experimentation – was harmonized for my existence, I can't help but question what this great experiment has done to me, to my family, and to all of us.

I'm blessed with the most beautiful mother-in-law. She is generous to a fault, always giving of herself to my wife, my children, and to me. As I think about how our habitats shape our behavior, I've taken note of how she impacts my family.

When we know my mother-in-law is stopping by, my wife will tidy up the house. It's not that our house is particularly messy, or that my mother-in-law would judge us lacking if it were, but more that my wife's respect and admiration for her mom makes her take note of the shape our home is in. It's one of those subtle things, a cue to the rest of the family.

I've watched how my two daughters burst with joy when their grandmother is around, how the affection she has for them is different from the way my wife and I interact with them. It's a different dimension of unconditional love and it has an important impact on the kids. And, of course, while my wife and I talk a lot, those conversations are very different than the ones she has with her mom. I'm incapable of providing my wife with the calming reassurance that one conversation with her mom can bring.

I've noticed changes in my own behavior. I'm a better man – I'm a better version of me – when my mother-in-law is around. I'm politer. I'm kinder. I'm less judgmental and more generous with my spirit. I find myself wanting to be a better person in her presence.

It's not lost on me that, if I had been born even a century earlier, there is a strong likelihood that my mother-in-law would be living with us, not in a house 15 miles away. If you asked me whether I want my mother-in-law living here, I – like nearly every modern American family – would say "no," yet it's clear to me that my children would be happier and more loved. My wife would maybe struggle a little but would likely feel more secure, more complete. And I'm confident that I would ultimately be a better person, that my low moments would be not-so-low, tempered by the daily influence of an extended family.

I'm not suggesting we should all live with our in-laws. There is a reason why, when given the choice, Americans opted for a different living arrangement. Living closely with others can be difficult. There is tension to be worked out. Disputes to be resolved. Many competing interests to be harmonized.

It would be difficult, yes, but would we be better for it? I don't know, but I suspect we might.

Moving to a Neighborhood

Ultimately my family moved from the cul-de-sac into an urban neighborhood a few blocks from my city's downtown. Moving from a neighborhood that I don't believe has a future to a 1914 home in a historic area was one way my family acted on the insights from my work with Strong Towns. Even so, it was a lifestyle choice as much as a financial decision.

At the old house, the girls were stuck biking the driveway, maybe the cul-de-sac. Anything unaccompanied beyond that risked tragedy with a speeding vehicle and a moment of inattention. And even if they had ventured further, there was no place to go. Their friends were likewise spread across the area, brought together outside of school only through scheduled play dates and long car rides.

The new neighborhood is full of kids. A city park is a mere block away. The girls have learned to navigate the neighborhood on their own, a life skill I took for granted yet few of their peers seem to possess. They can go to the store or the library or, when they scrounge up some money, downtown for an ice cream. I'm watching them grow into the kind of confident people I always hoped they would be.

The move has saved me five hours a week of commuting. Instead of being stuck behind the wheel, I walk or bike to work. And to get groceries. And to the hardware store. And anyplace else I can reasonably get to, even in the winter. I go days without driving, and I've felt myself become more relaxed, less stressed, as a result.

The most consequential change with the move has been adding neighbors to my life. I will acknowledge, having grown up on a farm without neighbors, and having watched some of my short-tempered uncles get in petty feuds with theirs, this was the thing I was most nervous about with the move. My apprehension could not have been more misplaced.

I live in Minnesota and it snows here in the winter, sometimes quite a bit. I'm responsible for shoveling the snow off the sidewalks in front of my house, but I often don't get the chance. Every time it snows, there is an informal race to be the friendliest neighbor and clear everyone's sidewalks. Very often, I'll go out with a shovel only to discover that mine are already cleared.

There's an elderly woman across the alley who offered to pay me to clear the snow from her driveway. I clear the snow, but no money changes hands. She keeps an eye on things, including my kids and my sometimes wandering dog. It's been more than a fair trade.

I'm an introvert who enjoys long walks alone, avoids social gatherings where possible, and can't remember names. None of that has kept me from getting to know all my immediate neighbors. It's almost impossible not to as we run into them all the time. I know their kids, their pets, and some of their plants. When we're out of town, they watch our house. We do likewise for them.

I'm not so naïve as to believe that all neighbors are wonderful, but mine are. They add a lot of joy to my life. And even if they didn't, they're helpful. Life can be a struggle; it's good to have someone right there helping. I imagine that the people who built my house more than a century ago felt similarly.

That is, if they even noticed. This is how humans had been building neighborhoods for as long as any of them could remember. It's possible they just took acting neighborly for granted. It was as expected a cultural practice as merging in traffic is to us.

A Good, Long Walk

I was part of an exchange program sponsored by Rotary International that sent me to Southern Italy back in the spring of 2000. I had never been out of the country, let alone to someplace so different from where I came from. The trip changed my life.

Part of the unique experience of being in Italy was, of course, the food. The team I was with all ate like royalty. Our various Italian hosts brought us out for what felt like a Thanks-giving-scale meal, twice a day, every day. Later in the trip when I was on my own, I ate an entire pizza every day for dinner and, when I learned the word for "French fries," added an order of them – fried in exquisite olive oil – to my regular diet. I've never eaten so much in a six-week period.

The other unique experience for me was walking. I came from a city, in a culture, where a trip longer than a block meant getting into a car. In Italy, we walked everywhere. They all did. It was the easiest way to get around and, since everyone walked most places, the cities were very delightful to walk in.

I'm six feet tall. When I arrived in Italy, I weighed 185 pounds, a weight slightly above where I should have been at that age but by no means overweight. When I left Italy six weeks later, despite eating a bizarre amount of food, I weighed a very heathy 165. I could talk about the value of the Mediterranean diet, but that wasn't it for me. It was all the walking.

All of us on the trip recognized the same effect. In fact, at one point we were sitting outside at a café watching people walk by when we decided to count the number of them who were obviously overweight. It was a busy street with at least a couple people walking by each minute. We were there about 30 minutes. Total count: zero.

This is not to say that Italians don't struggle with obesity – official statistics suggest that they increasingly do[1] – nor that the well-tailored clothing they tended to wear didn't have a slimming effect, but it's clear that the people living there walked a lot, and that the activity seemed to keep them slimmer than what we were used to experiencing in America.

Upon returning to the Central Minnesota lifestyle I was accustomed to, I not only quickly regained the weight, but over time added even more. Yet, when my family moved from the cul-de-sac to the neighborhood home, I experienced a similar slimming effect. I was not going to the gym to work out, but I was now walking and biking a lot as part of my daily routine.

My youngest daughter, Stella, went to a neighborhood school a mile away and we frequently biked there together. The weight started to come down, little by little, despite no real changes to my (notoriously poor) eating habits.

Public health is outside of my area of expertise, but it's hard not to entertain a connection between the new, experimental human habitat we've created and our national crisis with obesity. Heart disease, high blood pressure, and diabetes are all complex health conditions with multiple vectors of causation; I'm not attempting to argue otherwise. Even so, every time I've been to the doctor – for myself or with an elderly family member – the medical advice has always included daily physical activity.

The people who lived in my neighborhood a century ago walked multiple blocks – often many miles – as part of their everyday routine. Their ancestors would have done likewise. Today, it's not only possible but very likely that, without intentional effort, someone living in this same neighborhood would experience only a small fraction of that level of physical activity.

Humans are adapting to a new set of conditions, shifting into habitat we're not physiologically accustomed to. When we look at other species, we observe Darwin's merciless insights: Evolution occurs with the survival of those best adapted to changing conditions. What type of human is best adapted to a sedentary lifestyle? It's unclear, with our unique capacity to countermand death in many instances, how we will evolve under this new set of stresses.

My walking and biking also revealed to me the large number of people who walk because they have no other choice. When I was traveling at high speeds in my car, these people were mostly invisible to me. Now they are everywhere, and I'm astounded by their struggles.

Walking is a lifestyle for me. When it's pouring down rain, or when the temperature is below zero as it often is during Minnesota's winters, I have the choice to drive. Many of my neighbors do not. And as a professional running my own organization,

I also have job security. If I decide I'm working from home to avoid nasty weather, there are no negative ramifications. For my neighbors that work multiple part-time jobs at or near minimum wage – and I've now met many of them – even being late has ramifications.

Jeff Speck, author of *Walkable City: How Downtown Can Save America, One Step at a Time*, describes a good walk as one that is "useful, safe, comfortable, and interesting." As I ponder how these four elements in what Jeff calls his "General Theory of Walkability" apply to my town, I recognize how despotic for people not in an automobile we have made this formerly walkable place. That the change has come at such a great cost to our financial health and prosperity only makes it more disturbing.

Financial realities demand that we make our cities more walkable, but it seems more than possible that this act will also make our lives better in unpredictable ways. As Speck suggests in *Walkable City*:

> We must understand that the walkable city is not just a nice, idealistic notion. Rather, it is a simple, practical-minded solution to a host of complex problems that we face as a society, problems that daily undermine our nation's economic competitiveness, public welfare, and environmental sustainability.[2]

In fairly simple and straightforward ways, we can improve the financial health of our cities while improving people's lives. I've come to find that insight deeply satisfying.

Talking to Each Other

It's hard not to question how our national discourse has been impacted by this development experiment. I'm aware that recency bias may prejudice us to believe that things have never been worse, but even if they aren't catastrophic from a historical perspective, there is something that feels deeply broken about the way Americans speak to each other, especially on political issues.

Many have identified social media as a root cause. I don't want to discount that, especially since my own experience has demonstrated to me that the algorithms eagerly dispense a steady stream of distorted, inflammatory, and derisive information, regardless of who I follow and interact with. I have taken steps to expand the range of authentic voices I'm exposed to in my social streams, but the algorithms push intellectual junk food nonetheless. I've found it best to limit my own social media exposure.

I live in a small town, but I get to spend a lot of my time in major cities, interacting with thoughtful people on substantive issues. In the modern political landscape, I go back and forth between Red America and Blue America, enjoying aspects of both but not feeling fully comfortable in either. Prior to November of 2016, ignorance of the other was accompanied with a level of suspicion, even curiosity. Following the election of Donald Trump as president, suspicion has turned to contempt, derision, and sometimes outright hatred.

One of the common questions I find myself answering in both Americas is "Do they really believe . . . ," as if the complex, multi-faceted "us" stands across the abyss from the monolithic "them," geographic separation being the only thing keeping us from being debased, or worse, by the moral vacuousness of the other. Social media, and cable news, makes this experience more visceral, but there are reasons to suspect the core problem resides in how we have arranged ourselves.

In his book *The Big Sort: Why the Clustering of Like-Minded America Is Tearing Us Apart*, journalist Bill Bishop combines demographic data, election results, and research in human psychology to show how America is becoming more politically polarized. As Americans move around in the modern landscape, they are now able to self-sort into neighborhoods of people with similar ideological frameworks.

As people seek out the social settings they prefer – as they choose the group that makes them feel the most comfortable – the nation grows more politically segregated – and the benefit that ought to come with having a variety of opinions is lost to the righteousness that is the special entitlement of homogeneous groups.

We all live with the results: balkanized communities whose inhabitants find other Americans to be culturally incomprehensible; a growing intolerance for political differences that has made national consensus impossible; and politics so polarized that Congress is stymied and elections are no longer just contests over policies, but bitter choices between ways of life.[3]

The moral psychologist Jonathan Haidt suggests that Americans now live in "lifestyle enclaves" where they rarely encounter people with a different moral framework than their own. This has enormous ramifications for our discourse. When we don't hear opposing viewpoints presented authentically by people we know and respect, those beliefs are easily reduced, caricatured, and discounted.

This moves the median of accepted discourse in each enclave further to the extremes. A moderate opinion in an electorally blue city would be a radically left opinion in Red America. Conversely, a moderate opinion in a red precinct is offensive and heretical to those in Blue America. As Haidt explains in his book, *The Righteous Mind: Why Good People Are Divided by Religion and Politics*, this effect is universal across all political beliefs.

Morality binds and blinds. This is not just something that happens to people on the other side. We all get sucked into tribal moral communities. We circle around sacred values and then share post hoc arguments about why we are so right and they are so wrong. We think the other side is blind to truth, reason, science, and common sense, but in fact everyone goes blind when talking about their sacred objects.[4]

What is different today from what our ancestors would have experienced is the unnaturally filtered and curated interactions we have with those of a different moral framework. Cities have historically had people of both liberal and conservative dispositions; in such places it would have been impossible not to intimately know someone with whom one politically disagreed. Today such moral isolation is easy, perhaps even the default.

It's my contention that cities need both mind-sets to solve problems and thrive. Hierarchy without compassion for individual suffering quickly becomes tyranny. The liberal framework is critical to helping us understand where existing social structures create harm, and pushing society to update, sometimes even completely reimagine, those structures.

Yet, a society without a certain level of structure becomes chaotic, the destabilization creating deep psychological anxiety and tension. When conservatives advocate for certain institutions and traditions, they are – as Haidt has suggested – rightly pointing out that "you don't help the bees by destroying the hive."

The deep irony of the post-war development experiment is that it was largely a liberal-initiated destruction of the hive, wrapped in the language of both nationalism and justice, that has now grown to be sacred to conservatives. Untangling that gordian knot of culture is going to require deep intention, and huge doses of empathy, by those who grasp the urgency of the situation.

As an undergraduate, I identified with the Republican Party and called myself a conservative, even though I was more of a libertarian. This was during Bill Clinton's first administration and the Newt Gingrich–led Republican Revolution. Around 2002, halfway through George W. Bush's first term, I was invited to be a regular political commentator on a community radio station. We focused mostly on state politics but, of course, expanded our conversation as events warranted. I was introduced on-air as the "Republican" of the conversation.

Over time, particularly as my work with Strong Towns progressed and I found myself interacting with lots of people outside of my moral matrix, I eventually stopped clinging to culturally defined political labels and allowed my own beliefs to wander. In 2015, I was invited to speak on a panel titled "Bipartisan Placemaking: Reaching Conservatives" at the Congress for the New Urbanism in Dallas. I thought about my remarks and came up with this formulation that fits most closely with my view of the world:

> At the national level, I tend to be libertarian. Let's do a few things and do them very competently.
>
> At the state level, I tend to be a Minnesota version of conservative Republican. Let's devolve power, use markets and feedback where it drives good outcomes, and let's do limited state interventions when we have a broad consensus that things would be better by doing so. Let's measure outcomes and hold ourselves to a high standard.
>
> At the regional level, I tend to favor a more progressive approach. Let's cooperate in ways that improve everyone's lives. Let's work together to make the world more just.
>
> At the city level, I'm fairly progressive. What do we need to do to make this place work for everyone? Let's raise our taxes, and put sensible regulations in place, to make that a reality.
>
> At the neighborhood level, I'm pretty much a socialist. If there is something I have that you need, it's yours. All I ask is that you do the same in return, for me and my family.
>
> At the family level, I'm completely communal. Without hesitation, I'll give everything I have so my family has lives that are secure, happy, and prosperous. I expect nothing in return.

Knowing this, which of the two dominant political parties do I most closely align with? I don't think either one today, but if we went back a generation or two – or a hundred years – someone with my mind-set could have easily identified as a Republican or a Democrat. The parties themselves used to be far more intellectually diverse, less morally pure. I've presented this framework in front of many audiences and have always received positive feedback. In other words, I suspect my approach here is broadly representative of society. I believe that few of us are as rigidly orthodox in deed as our social feeds would suggest.

In *Why Liberalism Failed*, Patrick Deneen delves into the foundational assumptions of post-Enlightenment liberalism. His critique is the best explanation of the growing discontinuity between people, place, and politics that I have been exposed to. He suggests that central to the project of liberalism – which includes both left- and right-minded thinkers – is the elevation of the individual over the society, a condition that simultaneously elevates the centralized state.

> Individualism and statism advance together, always mutually supportive, and always at the expanse of lived and vital relations that stand in contrast to both the starkness of the autonomous individual and the abstraction of our membership in the state. In distinct but related ways, the right and left cooperate in the expansion of both statism and individualism, although from different perspectives, using different means, and claiming different agendas.
>
> The deeper cooperation helps to explain how it has happened that contemporary liberal states – whether in Europe or America – have become simultaneously more statist, with ever more powers and activity vested in central authority, and more individualistic, with people becoming less associated and involved with such mediating institutions as voluntary associations, political parties, churches, communities, and even family.
>
> For both "liberals" and "conservatives," the state becomes the main driver of individualism, while individualism becomes the main driver of the state.[5]

I still talk politics on the same community radio station, but I worked to change the format. The program I'm now on is a monthly show called *Dig Deep*, where, for an hour or more, I join with the liberally-minded Aaron Brown in an effort to identify common ground across our political divide. We both work hard to avoid cheap shots and flaming rhetoric – it's harder than it sounds – and we've committed intentional effort to understanding each other, even when we don't agree.

I think it's no coincidence that Aaron and I find we have the most agreement when it comes to what should happen at the local level. I'm convinced that, the more we shift our focus and energy to cities, towns, and neighborhoods, the more virtue we will find in each other, and the more we will accomplish.

A Life of Meaning

Most nights I take a walk with the family dog, a Shar-Pei/Lab mix named Gryffindor. We have a regular route we travel that takes us by St. Francis Catholic Church. This is the church my family attends. My parents go there. I remember sitting next to my grandparents, who went there when they were alive, as did my great-grandparents, whom I knew briefly as a young boy. I presume the two generations of Marohns prior to them helped build the church, which replaced a smaller one up the street.

My wife and I were married in that church and our kids were baptized there. In addition to weekly mass, I've attended many funerals and weddings, experiencing the highs and lows of life with family, friends, and passing acquaintances. Beyond the spiritual connection, the place has deep personal meaning for me.

I try to walk by it each day. I tend to slow down and look at it, shutting off whatever I'm listening to and intentionally putting myself in that place at that time. Sometimes I stop and sit on the steps. I've said prayers there by myself. I'm not going to suggest I'm a good Catholic or even a good Christian – they are both a struggle for me – but there is something about the regular, intentional contact that I have with that place, and all its meaning, that guides my heart in ways I'm grateful for.

I feel the same about the cemetery, which Gryffindor and I regularly walk through. My grandmother is buried there. She was a beautiful Norwegian woman who passed away during my senior year of high school; she was far too young. She lived in the neighborhood and when I went to grade school – the school my mother attended and then where my children also went – I used to walk over to her house for lunch on Fridays.

Grandma would feed me pizza, my favorite. For dessert, it was Twinkies – a coveted treat my practical mother would never buy – except at Christmas time, when she'd fill me full of krumkake and rosettes, two Norwegian cookies. Then we would just sit and talk.

I'm not sure what I believe about the afterlife, but I often stand at her grave and talk to her. I tell her spirit the good things of my life as well as the struggles. I tell her about my wife – whom she knew – and the kids, whom she never met. I'm not sure what impact this has on my soul, but grandmothers are there for listening and loving. In that way, she is still very much my grandmother.

In 2004, when I was running my engineering and planning firm, I received a call from a Hasidic Jew from Brooklyn, New York, named Moshe Landau. He had found my name doing an Internet search for "rural planner." Moshe wanted to know if I would come to Brooklyn to meet with him and his community about potentially building a new city for them in the middle of rural Kansas. Being unqualified for such an undertaking on virtually every level that mattered, I, of course, agreed to meet.

I'm from a part of America where religious diversity means Catholics *and* Lutherans, so I knew embarrassingly little about Jews and even less about the Hasidim. I ordered and read as many books as I could and, by the time I made the trip, had a thorough book understanding of the history of the Hasidim, their migration to America, their struggles in Brooklyn, specifically, and many of their religious beliefs and practices.

What I discovered instead was something no textbook could have revealed. The Hasidic in Brooklyn are a complex community of people who have chosen an intentional way of living together. In many ways, it embraces modernity – Moshe and I bonded over our passion for the show *24*, which was big at the time – but it also clings to the traditional. I found them beautiful and inspiring.

I know the Hasidim are controversial in New York. They live very different lifestyles than the typical New Yorker, even those who are Jewish. Due to their social structure, they tend to be an overly influential voting block (literally) when it comes to borough-level politics, a source of tension. Their approach to gender-relations, social hierarchy, and education are far outside of the modern mainstream. Still, as a Catholic who struggles with living my faith, here for the first time I was among people who had structured their place to reinforce the lives they desired to live. It had a large impact on me.

As we talked about the new city they wanted to create, they didn't seem to care about any of the practical things that an engineer or planner would concern themselves with. The things they impressed on me had to do with their community. They needed access to Kosher food for their table practices. They needed neighborhoods where they could walk to their worship places since they didn't drive on the Sabbath. They needed gathering places and social spaces that reflected their values and priorities.

I spent three days among them. I found many of their practices strange, but none without meaning. As time went on, I recognized that, if Moshe came and visited me, he would likely find the Catholic tradition odd, but he would be more perplexed by how it is undermined by the place in which it is embedded. That was the biggest difference between our lives.

I would never seek to structure my city to reinforce Catholic practices, nor would I recommend that any American city do so for any religious faith. Even so, I'm aware that neighborhoods of the past, and sometimes entire cities, were structured around such practices. In fact, when it comes to ancient cities, I'm unaware of any city that wasn't.

Chris Arnade worked for two decades as a bond trader before giving that up to devote himself to documenting the lives of the poor and those struggling with addiction. His photos and commentaries are moving in a way that challenges the comfortable. I had an opportunity to interview him for the *Strong Towns*

Podcast and asked what he thought the most important thing was that would improve the lives of the struggling people he met. His answer: religion.

Arnade went to pains to point out that he was not religious and that he wasn't suggesting that the poor and addicted find solace in mystical beliefs. Religion, in the context he was referencing, is the practice of community, of people coming together to help each other with the complex burdens of life. Some of these burdens are financial and physical, but many are deeply emotional. Such practices have been with humans since the beginning of recorded history. We are, in a sense, co-evolved to bind together in this way.

The United States is a secular nation, and as an American citizen, I am firmly committed that it remains that way. Even so, it's clear that as our religiosity fades, there is no cultural structure providing equivalent meaning and guidance for our lives. There is no common purpose, no unifying set of moral beliefs, that binds us together as people.

Some may argue that there is no consequence to this, but it's hard not to associate the reported rise in depression, loneliness, and suicide with a living arrangement that runs counter to our evolved nature. As Jonathan Haidt suggests:

> When I began writing *The Happiness Hypothesis*, I believed that happiness came from within, as Buddha and the Stoic philosophers said thousands of years ago. You'll never make the world conform to your wishes, so focus on changing yourself and your desires. But by the time I finished writing, I had changed my mind: Happiness comes from between.
>
> It comes from getting the right relationships between yourself and others, yourself and your work, and yourself and something larger than yourself.
>
> Once you understand our dual nature, including our groupish overlay, you can see why happiness comes from between. We evolved to live in groups.[6]

The only common cultural practice consistently reinforced by the structure of the places we've built today is consumption.

All around us, we're prompted to consume, to increase our desires beyond what we now have. This is contrary to the structure of prior societies, especially ancient ones, which acknowledged avarice but made self-denial a virtue, a path to inner peace.

Human habitat evolved to assist us in becoming a better member of the community, to nudge humans along a path of virtue. This goal is completely absent in modern conversations about building cities. For some individualists, even the suggestion is offensive.

What does it mean to "live a good life" in modern America? Beyond an individual's capacity to consume, it's unclear. Does a "good life" today have a moral dimension, one that involves sacrifice and self-denial for the benefit of others? Military journalist Sebastian Junger, who spent significant time reporting from the front lines of combat, suggests an answer in the structure of society.

> It's revealing, then, to look at modern society through the prism of more than a million years of human cooperation and resource sharing. Subsistence-level hunters aren't necessarily more moral than other people; they just can't get away with selfish behavior because they live in small groups where almost everything is open to scrutiny.
>
> Modern society, on the other hand, is a sprawling and anonymous mess where people can get away with incredible levels of dishonesty without getting caught. What tribal people would consider a profound betrayal of the group, modern society simply dismisses as fraud.[7]

I served in the Army and I found Junger's book *Tribe: On Homecoming and Belonging* deeply relevant to that experience. While there was a lot of hardship and difficulty involved, there are few things I've ever done that have been as rewarding or made me feel happier. I discussed this with my grandfather, a Marine veteran of World War II, and he felt the same: He experienced horror and trauma, but also felt a great deal of belonging, pride, and happiness. According to Junger:

> Human beings need three basic things in order to be content: they need to feel competent at what they do; they need to feel authentic in

their lives; and they need to feel connected to others. These values are considered "intrinsic" to human happiness and far outweigh "extrinsic" values such as beauty, money, and status.

Modern society seems to emphasize extrinsic values over intrinsic ones, and as a result, mental health issues refuse to decline with growing wealth. The more assimilated a person is into American society the more likely they are to develop depression during the course of their lifetime.[8]

Junger goes on to note that the Amish, who live as a community apart from American society, shunning nearly all modern conveniences, have "exceedingly low rates" of depression.

When I was visiting the Hasidic in Brooklyn, I stopped with Moshe at his apartment. He has a wife and three children and together they live in a place smaller than my college apartment. They are always intimately surrounded by other Hasidic Jews.

In their living room – which doubles as a bedroom overnight – there were two extra children in folding playpens. Moshe told me that his rabbi asked if he and his wife would take in these children for a while so a neighboring couple could work on their struggling marriage. I looked around the extremely cramped apartment and asked how long this was going to be. Moshe shrugged, "As long as they need, I guess."

My house has vastly more space than Moshe's, yet I can't imagine opening it up like that. Even more telling, I can't imagine being *asked* to do so. I don't even know where such a request would happen. It would require a frequency of contact, a level of intimacy, with people in my community that I just don't have.

When it comes to the people in my community, I am often asked to donate, but I'm rarely asked to give. Yet, at my own parish, we frequently sing a hymn written in honor of our namesake, Saint Francis, that includes the line "It is in giving of ourselves that we receive." These thoughts are not absent in our words, nor often in our deeds, but those actions require intentional struggle against the places we have built, places designed to suppress the intimacy of community.

There is a beautiful line in that *Prayer of Saint Francis* that I find myself often returning to. It has come to me as I finish this work.

O divine Master, grant that I may not so much seek
to be consoled as to console,
to be understood as to understand,
to be loved as to love.

Building a Strong Town requires that we seek not to be understood, but to understand each other. Not to be served, but to live as servants to those around us. We must receive the wisdom of our ancestors with humility and, with the same level of introspection and dedication to sacrifice, undertake the work of passing on a better place to subsequent generations. That is our burden.

It's also our path to salvation. Our cities are struggling financially, trapped in a system grinding them into decline. Working together in an intentional way, it is possible to make our places stronger financially while also improving the lives of people. That is the essence of a Strong Towns approach, the bottom-up revolution America desperately needs.

Notes

1. https://www.ncbi.nlm.nih.gov/pmc/articles/PMC5278644/.
2. Jeff Speck, *Walkable City* (New York: North Point Press, 2012).
3. Bill Bishop, *The Big Sort* (New York: Mariner Books, 2009).
4. Jonathan Haidt, *The Righteous Mind: Why Good People Are Divided by Religion and Politics* (New York: Vintage Books, 2012).
5. Patrick J. Deneen, *Why Liberalism Failed* (New Haven, CT: Yale University Press, 2018).
6. Jonathan Haidt, *The Righteous Mind: Why Good People Are Divided by Religion and Politics* (New York: Vintage Books, 2012).
7. Sebastian Junger, *Tribe* (New York: Hachette Book Group, 2016).
8. Ibid.

Afterword

In 2016, a group of Shreveport, Louisiana, city leaders and residents met with Charles L. Marohn, Jr. to discuss how our city could expand its capacity to self-correct through better policies and practices. As a result, our city and its culture have been changing daily.

As a river city, Shreveport thrived on the spoils of cotton and oil before supporting a strong middle class built primarily on the telecom and automotive industries. Neighborhoods sprung up around the industrial nuclei to create short commutes for workers. During this time, planners left room for growth around these nuclear points connected by Interstate 20. In more recent times, we have been a culture of drivers who watched our local downtown department stores evolve and relocate to upscale retail centers or malls.

Our history is complex and full of beautiful contradictions and painful moments that impact the decisions that have been made in regard to our development pattern over the last 60 years. Shreveport's core is a checkerboard of cultures and classes with historic neighborhoods patchworked together yet divided by commerce, highways, train tracks and our own psychology. Our population has transitioned from stagnant to declining as members of Generation X and Millennial cohorts leave to find opportunities in larger metropolitan areas. We are finding our way back to the core through the realization that we can no longer afford to acquire any more land and that we are at reckoning if we want to strengthen our city.

My group, ReForm Shreveport, began in 2016 as four friends on a mission to get Shreveporters to reconsider their relationship with the built environment. We host small group discussions about Strong Towns concepts. We tour the most productive parts of our city and discuss our failures and successes. We communicate with businesses about the potential of human-scaled retail and service sector development. We reach out to city leaders to encourage policy changes. We set goals to take on the "next small thing" that can make a big difference, just as Chuck encouraged us to do in the fall of 2016.

Our first project, which came just weeks after Chuck's visit, was to encourage walking in the neighborhood with the most walkability outside of downtown. The historic Highland neighborhood is adjacent to downtown and features a mix of grand homes dating back at least a century as well as modest, character-filled Craftsman bungalows crafted during the city's post-war boom. The tree-lined streets border blocks where some of the richest and poorest citizens in our city reside and, in some cases, live next door to each other. ReForm Shreveport began cleaning up the neighborhood's central park to increase usage and pedestrian accessibility. We partnered with a local permaculture influenced farmer to mitigate erosion and save trees. We gained the trust of the city's parks department by working with some intrepid public officials who helped with the park's beautification. We canvassed the neighborhood to learn how the residents around the park used it (not much) as well as their hope for a safer and more useful space that they would use more often. Highland Park sees many more visitors today than it saw five years ago.

Because of our efforts, more people are articulating not only their desire for change, but are dreaming bigger (or smaller?) than ever before as a result of learning the tools and the methods of cultivating a stronger town.

There comes a point where you understand policy and the role of the public in shaping policy so well that your friends see opportunities that you don't immediately see for yourself. Multiple friends suggested that I run for office. I finally heeded the call when I realized that we have an opportunity to push for sound decision making about how we shape our city for future generations. Thousands of people in my city want to encourage growth in our core and choose leaders who aren't afraid of making tough decisions to improve our infrastructure, encourage change, and show people what is possible if you just work to improve the next small thing within your purview. They elected me to city council at the end of 2018.

Shreveport is a work in progress, but we have good bones. City council members and members of our new mayor's administration often quote pieces of the Strong Towns message in council meetings. We have a number of projects in progress with different neighborhood groups looking to calm traffic on their streets and encourage bicycle and pedestrian activity. Not every project is perfect, not every implementation is as we might initially envision, but the dialogue and intent with which our community acts is beginning to evolve thanks in large part to the perspective we have gained through the visionary call to action that Chuck is instilling in cities and towns like ours across the country.

This can be your future too. Not a utopian society, but a society of communication and shared vision that values the human scale, the connection with neighbors, and the understanding of what being a community really means.

LeVette Fuller
Shreveport, Louisiana, council member

Acknowledgments

I would like to acknowledge the guidance and insights of Steve Mouzon, Jeff Speck, Andres Duany, Mike Lydon, Jason Roberts, and Monte Anderson. They have all added disproportionately to the insights contained in this book. I would also like to individually acknowledge John Anderson, whose friendship and counsel has gone beyond what I ever deserved. I will strive to pay it forward.

I would like to thank Jon Commers and Ben Oleson for their efforts in founding Strong Towns, and Justin Burslie for his critical help in the early days. The Blandin Foundation took an early gamble on us, a model of philanthropic leadership I admire and appreciate.

I am also extremely grateful for the stewardship – and friendship – of Andrew Burleson, Ian Rasmussen, and John Reuter in running the organization. So many great ideas were hatched with them while standing in line at theme parks. Strong Towns would not have accomplished much without them.

I also want to acknowledge my co-conspirators at Urban3, Joe Minicozzi and Josh McCarty. The sleepless nights and long car rides geeking out together have become tales of legend. May there be many more.

I'm also grateful for the team at Strong Towns, especially Rachel Quednau, Kea Wilson, Michelle Erfurt, Daniel Herriges, Bo Wright, Jacob Moses, and Missy Trees. They always picked up the slack when my late nights writing wore me down. Churros for everyone!

Thank you to Quint Studer and Dottie DeHart for the support and for nudging me to write this book.

And I want to thank my mentors, George Orning and Stuart Lade, for everything they did to push me along this path in life. I'll never repay the debt.

About Strong Towns

Strong Towns is an international movement that's dedicated to making communities financially strong and resilient.

For generations, North American communities have been growing – or at least, they've been building. But as we've paved endless roads, raised countless buildings, and put more and more infrastructure in the ground, we've given almost no thought to whether future generations will be able to afford to maintain the world we'll leave them with – or how many of the things we build are making our communities worse places to live today.

The Strong Towns approach is a radically new way of thinking about the way we build our world. We believe that in order to truly thrive, our cities and towns must:

- Stop valuing efficiency and start valuing resilience.
- Stop betting our futures on huge, irreversible projects, and start taking small, incremental steps and iterating based on what we learn.
- Stop fearing change and start embracing a process of continuous adaptation.
- Stop building our world based on abstract theories and start building it based on how our places actually work and what our neighbors actually need today.
- Stop obsessing about future growth and start obsessing about our current finances.

But most importantly, we believe that Strong Citizens from all walks of life can and must participate in a Strong Towns approach – from citizens to leaders, professionals to neighbors, and everyone in between.

Strong Towns, the 501(c)(3) organization, is working to make the Strong Towns approach real in every city and town in North America. Through producing media, hosting events, and by networking people together, the messaging is spreading, and places are beginning to change.

To learn more about Strong Towns, or to support the movement, go to www.strongtowns.org.

Get Involved in the Strong Towns Movement

Here's how:

EXPLORE the universe of content produced by Strong Towns media that keeps you asking hard questions about how we build today, and shines a spotlight on a better way that we must take up tomorrow, at strongtowns.org.

SUBSCRIBE to the Strong Towns email list for important updates, top stories from Strong Towns media, and notifications about when Charles L. Marohn, Jr. will be in your area. (strongtowns.org/email).

CONNECT with The Strong Towns Network of readers, members and advocates around the world. Get the inspiration, resources, and relationships you need to make your community stronger. Visit strongtowns.org/connect for more information.

EXPERIENCE the Strong Towns message live in person. For a full schedule of in-person events presented by Charles L. Marohn, Jr. and other members of the Strong Towns team, visit strongtowns.org/events.

HOST a Strong Towns event in your place. Visit strongtowns.org/speaking for rates and details.

JOIN THE MOVEMENT. Become an official member of the Strong Towns movement at strongtowns.org/membership. Your contribution of any amount helps us produce the content, events, and platforms for connection that we need to change the way America is built—and that our communities need to make the Strong Towns approach the default.

About the Author

Charles L. Marohn, Jr. – known as "Chuck" to friends and colleagues – is the founder and president of Strong Towns. He is a professional engineer licensed in the State of Minnesota and a land use planner with two decades of experience. He holds a bachelor's degree in civil engineering and a master of urban and regional planning, both from the University of Minnesota.

Marohn is also the lead author of *Thoughts on Building Strong Towns – Volume 1*, *Volume 2*, and *Volume 3*, as well as the author of *A World Class Transportation System*. He hosts the *Strong Towns Podcast* and is a primary writer for Strong Towns' web content. He has presented Strong Towns concepts in hundreds of cities and towns across North America. He is featured in the documentary film *Owned: A Tale of Two Americas*, and was named one of the 10 Most Influential Urbanists of all time by Planetizen.

Marohn is a long-time commentator on KAXE Northern Community Radio. He currently co-hosts KAXE's *Dig Deep* program, a monthly examination of public policy issues affecting Minnesotans.

Chuck grew up on a small farm in Central Minnesota. The oldest of three sons of two elementary school teachers, he joined the Minnesota National Guard on his seventeenth birthday during his junior year of high school and served for nine years. In addition to being passionate about building a stronger

America, he loves playing music, is an obsessive reader, and religiously follows his favorite team, the Minnesota Twins.

Chuck and his wife live with their two daughters in their hometown of Brainerd, Minnesota.

Index

Page numbers followed by *f* and *t* refer to figures and tables, respectively.